D1625305

a better woman

a better woman

A MEMOIR

Susan Johnson

WASHINGTON SQUARE PRESS
PUBLISHED BY POCKET BOOKS
New York   London   Toronto   Sydney   Singapore

A Washington Square Press Publication of
POCKET BOOKS, a division of Simon & Schuster, Inc.
1230 Avenue of the Americas, New York, NY 10020

Copyright © 1999 by Susan Johnson

Originally published in Australia in 1999 by Random House Australia

ISBN: 0-7434-3296-7

First Washington Square Press hardcover printing April 2002

10 9 8 7 6 5 4 3 2 1

WASHINGTON SQUARE PRESS and colophon are
registered trademarks of Simon & Schuster, Inc.

For information regarding special discounts for bulk purchases,
please contact Simon & Schuster Special Sales at 1-800-456-6798
or business@simonandschuster.com

Lines from Katherine Gallagher's poem 'Firstborn' have been reproduced
with permission, courtesy of Katherine Gallagher. Lines from Celine's
Journey to the End of Night have been reproduced with permission,
courtesy of Calder Publications. During the production of this book,
the publisher has made every effort to trace permission for other extracts
reproduced in this publication.

Printed in the U.S.A.

To my three dearest boys, Les, Caspar and Elliot,
my parents John and Barbara Johnson,
and to the turning of the wheel

Contents

Perhaps a better woman after all,
With chubby children hanging on my neck
To keep me low and wise.

ELIZABETH BARRETT BROWNING,
AURORA LEIGH

Between my finger and my thumb
The squat pen rests.
I'll dig with it.

SEAMUS HEANEY,
DIGGING

Foreword

There is an advertisement appearing on television here in Melbourne as I write extolling the benefits of a certain breakfast cereal. In the ad several attractive young women, beautifully career-suited, moneyed, some with perfectly mannered children, speak confidently and boastfully about how they successfully manage to control their own lives.

Speaking straight to the camera, they tell us that this sense of control starts from their bodies up. In other words, if you can successfully control what goes into your body, how it is exercised, watered and fed, then you have taken the first crucial step towards self mastery.

It's my body, it's my life is the message and I once believed this myself. Until my body failed me, I too believed myself captain of my ship, mistress of everything I surveyed. I am a fully-fledged member of an arrogant generation, schooled in the notion of rights.

My generation believed in the right to control our own bodies, the right to have a baby if we wanted one, whether or not we lived with other women or with our child's father or on our own. We believed completely in inventing our own reality, that whatever we wanted we had an inalienable right to get.

In short, we pretty much believed we had a right to anything and were in complete control of every damn thing.

These days, I am not so sure about inalienable rights and absolute control. These days, everything good in my life strikes me as a blessing, a fragile, happy gift held in trust. I have no idea how I came by these blessings, nor when or if they will be taken away again, but I certainly know that it is not my will alone which holds them.

My swaggering days, you see, are well and truly over.

This book, like all books, is composed of half truth and half lie. The lie dwells in the gathering together, in the shaping of lived experience and the clearing of dross. Real life is full of dross, the plod of maintenance, and much of it is lived in the dark. Although this book is not fiction, it shares fiction's pruning and shaping and therefore cannot hope to offer you my naked self laid bare.

Besides, as I came to write it, I discovered things about my own writing I did not know. I discovered, for example, that although I had long believed that my writing was a process by which I brought the world closer, making everything more real or at least more understandable, more *mine*, this was not always the complete truth.

I found this out the night before I was to undergo an operation in which my stomach was to be sliced open and a section of bowel brought to the surface through which I was afterwards meant to expel faeces.

In one flash on that fearful night I suddenly saw that instead of bringing reality closer, my writing was acting as a buffer zone between reality and me. I had always thought my work was an exposure, a peeling back, but I understood then that I was recording what was happening to me as a way of stepping outside the reality of waking up the next afternoon with a bag of shit stuck to my belly.

And as well as this, which may surprise you given the nature of this book, I am paranoid about my privacy. I hate people knowing my business, I hate being the subject of speculative, idle gossip and, above all (and this is where the writer's egomaniacal dream of control comes in), I hate it when people get the story wrong.

I have such a strong regard for my own privacy, together with a morbid fear of being pitied, that some of my close friends will be learning for the first time in these pages the full story of what happened to me after the birth of my sons.

I did not wilfully deceive them. It was just that I could hardly bear to have been such a failure at having a baby, an event in human life we know to be both ordinary and extraordinary but which we mostly take to be a commonplace. An emergency temporary colostomy as a result of giving birth does not feature anywhere in our romanticised imagery of new mothers and babies triumphantly awash in flowers, breast milk and champagne.

Frankly, I was also uncomfortable talking about the mechanics of pooing into a plastic bag. I did not want people staring at my stomach in an attempt to locate a lump; I did not want people to unconciously move away from me. One or two of the few people I told did exactly that.

If I could not talk to my friends then (or, in one particularly painful period, to my husband), I could write everything down in the cheap red and black Chinese notebook I had bought in London when I was first deliriously pregnant. As always in my life, my writing was my confessional, my salvation, my buffer zone and perhaps even my life raft.

The same book which recorded my terrors over the colostomy had also captured my tentative forays into imagining myself a mother and, later, after Caspar's birth, my son's feed times, and hastily scribbled descriptions, such as how I found his first tooth accidentally one morning: it felt like a tiny, frilled shell beneath my finger.

For months and months I did not write in my book at all because I lived as if beneath the sea. Every now and again I would surface from that sleepless, exhausting round of feeding Caspar, changing him, soothing him, washing his nappies, to see that the season had changed or to notice with a shock that my son no longer looked like a newborn baby.

Nonetheless, that same scribbled red and black book forms the skeleton of this story. You may be wondering by now why someone who purports to be as protective of her privacy as I am would then allow that story to be published in a book revealing intimate details about the failings of her vagina. My answer to that lies in the same place as my inability to disclose such details face to face with my friends: only in my writing am I free to express the unutterable.

Only writing allows me to glimpse the quivering of my own consciousness. Only writing allows me the freedom to be shameless, to exist without reserve, oblivious to consequence. Paradoxically, too, only writing allows me the privacy of my own thoughts, the setting free of everything I know without censorship or boundaries. If you met me face to face I could not begin to describe to you the shape of the place I have been but my writing could do it.

As such, I cannot regard this book as embarrassingly confessional, and certainly not brave as some have suggested. It exists simply because I am a writer and writing to me is like breathing. I did not become a writer as a career option; writing things down is the only way I know of existing.

Whether or not I need to publish my personal findings (or indeed whether anyone will be interested) is of course an entirely different matter. Here I offer you such reasons as money to feed myself and my children, an interested publisher who originally thought she was going to get a writer's journal about the first year of motherhood but ended up with something else entirely, plus a desire on my part to bring to light the experience of one woman and mother because our stories have long been dismissed as trivial and 'only' domestic. If my particular story has resonance for just one reader I shall be happy.

So, you see, a book composed of half truth and half lie. As the teller of the tale I have revealed only those details I wish you to know. I have already confessed to you about the lying part but I hope there is truth here too. My own truth, certainly, glimpsed only briefly, *en passant*, on its way to becoming something else but still truth of a kind.

Because there are other people besides myself involved in this story there are other versions of truth I have necessarily left out. While I am free to write about myself I am not free to write about my husband or my sons. My husband would undoubtedly offer you another kind of truth, but his version (with his agreement) will largely go unrecorded here. Les was there but back at camp, so to speak, while I was hunkered down in a ditch at the front line.

I will tell you however that he had serious doubts about my publishing this book at all. These doubts had to do with his belief that no-one wants to know the bad stories about pregnancy and childbirth, that no-one really wants to hear about what can go wrong, and that by publishing such a story I was placing myself directly in the line of fire.

He worried that, like the New Age philosophies which blame the cancer patient for getting cancer, readers would be quick to find a reason why I had brought such a catastrophe upon myself, as a way of distancing themselves from the thought of such a catastrophe ever happening to them. He said people were quick to assign the label 'loser', in an unconscious urge to isolate the grotesque from their midst.

Here I stand anyway, your worst nightmare, bringing back news from the pit.

I want to reassure anyone reading this who is pregnant or contemplating having a baby that what happened to me happens to very few women. Births resulting in recto-vaginal fistulas are virtually unheard of in the western world today, and Australian surgeons specialising in the condition are likely to see perhaps three or four cases a year. My own doctor has treated only a handful of such women. It is the women of the third world, giving birth without recourse to stitches and sterile conditions who continue to suffer fistulas. Most Australian women only know what a fistula is because of a television documentary on the work of the Australian gynaecologist Catherine Hamlin in Ethopia.

For a middle-class woman of the first world to be left with a minuscule passage running between the vagina and rectum following a repair of a third-degree tear is extraordinary bad luck. For a further repair of that fistula to fail, resulting in a temporary colostomy, is a worst-case scenario.

Thankfully, the vast majority of babies born in the west are delivered safe and whole, and their mothers with them. The human body is an astonishing thing and the wonder of it can be witnessed in those myriad births where the muscles and nerves and heart work gloriously together to bring a child to light and to leave a mother unscathed. I have a new respect for the body (and a new cold fear) which I certainly did not have before I gave birth.

But I have to warn you I have also learnt that giving birth brings a woman the closest she will ever come to the tender heart of life. Life and death will be right in the room with you, you will feel life's breath upon your face and know the throb of life's blood.

You will sense for a moment the meaning of existence, how fragile the membrane is between life and death, and then the curtains will close again on life's mystery and you will be left with only the vaguest dream.

These then are my memories, my vague dreams, half truths and half lies. Reader, here are some things which happened.

Getting Ready to Fall

When we are green, still half-created, we believe that our dreams are rights, that the world is disposed to act in our best interests, and that falling and dying are for quitters. We live on the innocent and monstrous assurance that we alone, of all the people ever born, have a special arrangement whereby we will be allowed to stay green forever.

TOBIAS WOLFF,
THIS BOY'S LIFE

The year that I turned thirty-five, my arms began to feel empty. I remember a moment when I was sitting behind my lover in a car driving through France, staring at the back of his head. Everybody in the car was talking but all I was conscious of was a longing in my empty arms to form themselves into that ancient female crook and cradle a baby.

I was living in Paris then, and my sixtyish, childless painter friend Simone confirmed that this longing first struck the body. 'My own body did not need it,' she said in English, without sentiment or regret. 'You must find out if yours does.'

My lover was an Italian–American who spoke heavily accented French. His character had a large dose of American schmaltz and an Italian love of drama, and inside his head were screened private soaps in which he imagined himself as the war/foreign correspondent who finally settles down with a difficult but artistic Australian.

He cried easily and was terribly kind. He had thin lips and when I first kissed them I imagined myself falling into a kind of black abyss. I had separated from my English husband and left Hong Kong only a short time before and was not sure I wanted to kiss anyone.

I told him this but it only increased his ardour. The less available I was the more he wanted me, and it took days, weeks and months for him to convince me that his hands bore no weapons and that his fleshless lips opened into softness. With one finger I traced a line down his flesh and was surprised to find his skin's tenderness.

Perhaps because I found myself hopeless I was writing a novel about hope. I lived in a large room with a tiny kitchen and a shower installed in a kind of cupboard. The room was off one of Paris's poorer streets and when I lay in bed I could clearly hear my neighbour's stream of piss hit the bowl of the toilet above me.

I tried to forget my lost husband as best I could but pain often roared in my chest. Yet paradoxically I was often exhilarated, when words rushed down my arm and out my blue pen, when I sipped a *café crème* and happened to look up at the dusty Paris sky. At times I even felt lucky.

My lover and I often talked of children even though we were virtual strangers. Once he sobbed in bed late at night when he spoke of the mutilated bodies of children he had seen in a river in El Salvador. I held him and my small room was crowded with our mutual terror.

I had never thought of myself as someone capable of ever having children. I thought it was what normal people did, people whose bodies and hearts and minds functioned in a way mine did not.

This conviction arose, in the first place, from an awareness that my body was not like everyone else's. My mother and I still dispute this, but I say I was aware of the hole in my chest as early as six, when I fell off a fishing wall onto rocks covered with oyster shells and had to take off most of my clothes so my rescuers could get to the wounds.

In my version I remember trying desperately to cling onto my shirt to cover my terrible flaw: between my flat nipples there was a large hole, as though God punched his clenched fist into me before he let me out. I already knew that no other children, including my two younger brothers, had this imperfection and that it somehow marked me.

I remember standing in the sun holding in front of me a blue Hawaiian shirt while fresh blood streamed down my arms. There was blood on my legs, on my face, in my eyes, but all I was worried about was hanging onto the shirt so that no-one would see how different I was, that I was not a normal girl.

Even years later, after I turned sixteen and the hole was repaired by breaking my sternum and re-setting it with a steel pin, I never felt myself to be like everyone else.

Now that my sons are here I sometimes find myself watching too carefully the flare of bones in their tiny boys' chests, on the lookout for the smallest hint of collapse.

I believe now that the bones which formed me physically formed me in other ways too. Many people who grow up into writers experience themselves as different, left on the sidelines by illness, physical uniqueness, tragedy, some profound notion of their own solitariness. Only children often become writers, children from toxic marriages, children whose interior worlds somehow became more radiant than the regular world witnessed by eyes.

I believe now that I wrote myself into life. Before I learnt how to do it I lived as if blind, forever raging against the dark. Learning how to write illuminated life itself for me, letting me see fully for the first time its shape and dimensions.

Before I learnt to write I did not know who I was. I was young, of course, but back then it always seemed that I was living in the wrong place, with the wrong people. I remember miserable early years living with a man who was totally unsuitable for me and sharing a house with his politically active friends. It was the late 1970s; I was nineteen, twenty; everyone else was closer to thirty and appeared to know everything.

I would sit in our room trying to get the courage up to say something at a meeting, or even at dinner, but whenever I was in a room filled with people having a discussion about the banning of street marches in Queensland I noticed the wrong things. I noticed that a woman had been crying, for example, or that someone's hands shook or that so-and-so appeared to have an unrequited crush on the dark, good-looking man in the corner. In other words, I was a writer. I was a witness to the small, unspoken gestures which reveal felt life, I was in love with the idea of making sense of everything I saw.

I did not yet know how to write but I was already full of yearning. I felt strangled by inarticulateness, choked up with all the million things I wanted to say and it was only when I held a pen in my hand that I felt soothed and the world became untangled. I longed to grab life by the throat and wrest it into some kind of beautiful pattern so that other people might recognise the weave. I wanted to move people in the same way I had been moved by books which illuminated the experience of being alive and breathing. I wanted to write the truest things I knew.

I see now that I also wished to create or invent myself. I do not understand how other people can live their lives without this. For me, living without writing, without trying to make messages from chaos, would be like living in exile from the deepest part of myself.

It seemed to me that my body grew older faster than the rest of me. At thirty-five I sometimes still imagined myself a young girl bursting free, smashing imaginary fathers and impossible husbands and any-thing else which stood in my way. I was embarrassingly *unmade* on the inside, still groping on the water's edge while my same-aged friends had long ago swum away.

If at thirty-five I knew without a doubt that writing was to be my life's work, I was less confident about my ability to love and be loved in return. I remember being stung when my Paris lover remarked that my books were way ahead of me and it was vital that I catch up.

I secretly looked upon my best friend Emma in Brisbane as a

grown-up, with her long-time husband, her two children, her steady, everything-in-place life. She had a proper house and a car, living-room furniture: she knew what she would be doing from one month to the next.

I thought of women who had given birth as having passed through one of life's most crucial doors, mothers somehow rendered unable to reveal the secrets they had found on the other side to those non-mothers who had not passed through.

The year I turned thirty-five I began to sense clumsily that I must find a way to move forward into the second half of my life, to find a way to grow up properly. I certainly did not believe that the only way of doing this was by having a child, I only knew that I had come to the end of myself. It was clear even to me that the old way of being myself was no longer working and that unless I wanted to spend the rest of my life emotionally atrophied I had better act.

Meanwhile, my body had its own plans. All the while I was trying to compose a mature intellectual and rational framework in which to answer the question of whether or not to have a child, my body believed it already had the solution. I felt like a fruit ready to burst, ripe with longing: I was pure sensation, physical craving, tangible as hunger or thirst. My body was yearning to be taken over, filled up, my blood longed to feed a living thing not itself.

No matter how hard I tried to think about the effect a child would have on my life and work (and I believed very seriously in Cyril Connolly's dictum that 'the pram in the hall' was chief among the enemies of promise) I could not calm the clamouring in my veins.

I thought of all the woman writers throughout history who had not had children, and it seemed to me that childless woman writers vastly outnumbered those with children. I did not know if having a child would mean the end of my creative life, if a single, irreversible act of physical creation would imperil my inner creative self. My writing *was* myself, my writing had made me and I did not know who I would be without it.

I remembered too how I had believed for a long time that having a child meant the end of your active life, shutting forever the door to adventure, to daring, to chance.

I knew without doubt that children were messy, noisy, sometimes boring, that they ate up your time, your energy, your very core and yet ... and yet ... I wanted one. I wanted something difficult and all-consuming, something powerful and obliterating, some experience of life I could not walk away from.

In short, I wanted to feel the weight of life. It seemed to me that I had always floated above life, above commitment, above responsibility, that I had somehow failed to enmesh myself in the fabric of living. As Doris Lessing wrote of herself in her autobiography, in words that also happened to fit me, I had 'rejected the human condition, which is to be trapped by circumstances'.

And, as if all this wanting wasn't enough, I also wanted the right man to make my imaginary baby with. I wanted love with which to knit our child, soft kisses and warm skin to make his bones. I wanted a baby to grow from the strength and wrap of my lover's arms, an organic offshoot of happiness.

Of course I see now that all this wanting, such a terrible blind urge to be pregnant and loved, carried with it the seeds of disaster as well as of redemption. In a novel by Diane Johnson, a character is described as being 'one of those people whose lives progress like one of those charts of heart attack, serrated peaks and valleys like shark's teeth'.

My life is like that: I got my baby made out of tenderness and a peak higher than clouds, but I also got a husband who feels he did not get as much choice about a baby as he should have. I got my baby knitted with love but I also got a badly broken body and a valley far, far from light.

When I married my first husband on a rainy day in London, my lips trembled. I had starved myself the month before and had practised saying the registry office words over and over. I thought they would halt in my mouth on the day, but they came out entirely whole.

Afterwards we went to a swank London hotel with my best friend Emma's aunt and cousins. Emma's aunt, a psychotherapist, had already tried to warn me off marrying someone I had known only three months but I wanted love to split me open and I heard nothing but the roar of want in my ears.

I had already had a bad falling out with another friend in Australia who had written to suggest that we have the honeymoon without getting married. *How dare you?* I wrote back. *Have I ever told you how to run your life?*

I was so convinced I was doing the right thing I would have killed anyone who had tried to stop me. All my instincts were telling me it was right, every nerve and muscle and fibre in my body screamed out that my husband was going to be my husband for the rest of my life.

In Hong Kong six months later a voice inside me tried to announce I had been wrong. I immediately stilled it, but I was flooded with shame, horrified by what was to come.

If my own instincts were so wrong, how could I trust anything again? You can see, can't you, how willing I have been to risk everything, to believe in the one, shining redemptive act. My friend Emma once said she admired above all my ability to take risks, but if daring to leave the safe world of nice, responsible men, of full-time work, the world of sick pay, holiday pay and mortgages had led me to the charm of a tiny rented flat in Paris, holidays in friends' houses in Corsica, whirlwind romances with unsuitable men and a writing life which I mostly loved, it had also led me to broken relationships and relative poverty (those old peaks and valleys). Many times (and more recently than I care to remember) I literally had only a few dollars to my name and I questioned the wisdom of leaping.

I think in many ways I have been an impulsive child, oblivious as any three year old playing catch by the road, heedless of the speeding traffic in her ecstatic dash for the ball.

My first husband and I had quickly spoken of babies. We had identically crooked eyeteeth and the very first night we had dinner together in Paris we joked that so would our children.

I was thirty-two then, and in reality children seemed to me a long way off. In reality I suffered a kind of psychic terror every time I thought seriously of children. It seemed to me that whatever I was made of was not strong enough to bear it, either physically or emotionally.

I was not yet ready either to relinquish the stage, to gladly pass the torch to those coming up from behind. If secretly I felt I could not yet handle the responsibility of children, I also felt a mean-spirited urge to keep hogging the light. *My* life was still unfurling, I was still having trouble imagining myself fully grown, let alone imagining someone else's growing.

In short, as I'm sure you will agree, I was remarkably self-centred, emotionally stranded somewhere around adolescence. Is it any wonder that my marriage began to fall apart around my head, that my husband and I began to squabble like the children we were? Some readers (and the occasional friend) think of my novels as my life served up re-heated, but I know my actual life is not shaped like fiction at all. My books are my means of ordering the world to attention: in real life husbands never go in the direction I want them to go and I can never see well enough in the dark.

At some point after I left my husband I slunk back to Australia. If I had been able I would have told no-one of my return and never set foot outside the door, so total was my sense of humiliation. For the first time in my life I felt that I was fundamentally broken and might never heal, that whatever old tricks I had used before to get myself to stand up again were no longer of any use.

Amazingly, I kept writing the novel about hope while all hope inside me was extinguished. While I felt my old self to be effectively dead I kept doggedly writing about a boy whose hopeful innocence saved him.

At some point I went back to Paris again and took up with the Italian–American lover who tried to convince me I was not dead. I believe his own grief was attracted to mine and that he thought he could save me.

I no longer remember the exact steps I took in my growing-up journey. I know only that it had something to do with the collapse of my first marriage and the great jolt that gave me, along with the kindness of my Italian–American lover, even though I subsequently learned that he loved me best when I was grief-stricken and far away, and that when I turned my face towards him he grew afraid.

It had to do, too, with long nights by myself where I stared down my own aloneness and dared imagine that I might be growing old. Somehow I began to feel that I had passed through barren land to end up in a place where I was comfortable enough to invite other people (even a baby) in.

By the time I met in London the Australian man who was to become my second husband, I felt both larger and smaller, calmer and certainly humbler. I no longer saw my life as an endless vista opening eternally before me.

A woman friend of roughly the same age as me had died of AIDS contracted through heterosexual sex, and I had gone through a crazy time of projecting my inner fears onto something outer, even convincing myself at one stage that I too had contracted AIDS, no matter how impossible, no matter how many tests I had which proved otherwise, no matter that a small rational part of me knew all along that I was being wildly irrational. Yet somehow I managed to come out the other side, finally able to experience myself as a fully-grown, middle-aged woman.

By the time I met my second husband I was ready for a baby and, just before I turned thirty-eight, several months after we were married, my body finally got its reward.

In no pregnancy book I read then or since was there a description of what was about to happen to my body. If my body had been impatient for metamorphosis, it was about to undergo its greatest crisis, in a catastrophic change more akin to decay than to fruition.

If I had known then what giving birth was to cost me, would I have ever dared to fall pregnant?

Yes, yes. A thousand times, yes.

Even now, remembering all the pain and suffering I have lived through, I would go through it all again. Even now, knowing that the freakish outcome of Caspar's birth was to make me feel like a freak all over again, I have never once wished him away. Every day I count myself lucky to have him.

I have felt the full weight of life upon me.

2

Metamorphosis

For years I dreamt you
my lost child, a face unpromised.
I gathered you in, gambling,
making maps over your head.
You were the beginning of a wish

KATHERINE GALLAGHER,
FIRSTBORN

I did not believe I was really pregnant, still less that I was capable of delivering to the world a living, breathing child with a proper head, a body, two arms and two legs. So entrenched in me was the idea that I was faultily made, I could not imagine anything emerging from my body which was not faulty as well. I had suffered an excruciatingly painful miscarriage only months before, and expected blood every time I looked down. This time, when two distinct blue stripes on the home pregnancy testing kit had revealed I was once again pregnant, I did not scream with joy and do a war dance around the house but sat soberly on the edge of the bath, holding the test in my hands.

Early days, I told myself, *so far to travel.*

Besides Les, I dared not tell anyone I was pregnant, believing superstitiously that if I counted my chickens before they hatched, they might not hatch at all. Yet despite the earlier miscarriage I could not help feeling lucky.

But before my baby even had a chance to reveal his shape in my belly, great questions began to be asked about him.

On my first visit to the young female doctor in Greenwich, where we were living, she asked whether I wished to consider genetic testing. I was about to turn thirty-eight and the risk of delivering a baby with a chromosomal abnormality (mainly Down's Syndrome) increases with maternal age.

There were a number of options open to me, she explained in a cool professional voice, and I remember trying not to stare too closely at photographs of her own whole, safely delivered children.

All non-invasive tests such as blood tests and the like, she went on, could only indicate probabilities, while the invasive tests such as Chorionic Villus Sampling (CVS) and amniocentesis gave definite answers but carried a 1 per cent to 2 per cent chance of miscarriage. I looked at her. Having already gone through one miscarriage I dared not risk another.

'And how does the chance of miscarriage compare with the chance of having a Down's Syndrome baby?'

She looked back at me. 'I think the chance of having a miscarriage as a result of invasive tests is slightly higher, but they're pretty comparable,' she replied.

Something must have registered on my face, something of the anguish and panic and longing raging inside me, because she immediately looked away again and began riffling around in her desk.

'I just got something the other day about this new, non-invasive test which is part of a research project at King's College. Ah, here we are,' she said, pulling a brochure from the drawer and running a finger down a line of figures. 'You're 38, aren't you?' she went on without waiting for my reply. 'According to this there's a 1 in 165 risk of fetal chromosomal abnormality.'

I sat there, between a rock and a hard place, momentarily swept of questions.

'I suppose it all comes down to how you view disability,' the doctor went on. 'Some women would rather risk a miscarriage than give birth to a disabled child. They don't think they could cope, it's as simple as that. They have no qualms, either, about terminating a pregnancy if the tests reveal an abnormality.

'Other women don't want to risk an invasive test which could endanger a perfectly healthy fetus. They'd rather take the chance and have the baby, disabled or not, than have no baby at all.'

I sat there, famous amongst my friends as one of life's big risk takers, wishing someone who was bigger than me would come into the room and tell me what to do. I had lost completely any taste I ever had for gambling.

It was the first time in my entire adult existence I found myself up against life itself, the big mystery at the centre of us all. I have already told you I was a late developer, and I had managed to get to almost forty without death or destruction fingering me directly; I harboured no thwarted wishes, no sense that life had ever said no to me. Even the miscarriage I regarded as a temporary setback and never once imagined it to be my last chance. As you know, I had also suffered personal failures, broken hearts and lost husbands, but I cannot say I ever felt I had been denied what I truly wanted. Even my failures I knew I had something to do with, even if I could not have said exactly what I had done to bring about my undoing at the time. I am embarrassed to say that up until that moment in the doctor's surgery, I believed myself to be the supreme architect of my own life.

Now, for the first time, I realised it was not my will alone which was setting the agenda, but fate, the cosmos, God, life itself: at any rate, something far greater and infinitely more powerful than myself. *I* might have decided it was time to have a baby, but the eggs inside my body had their own private timetable and had already grown weary of waiting. The question of whether they were past their use-by-date was entirely out of my hands.

It was my first inkling of what lay ahead of me: any sense I had of being in complete control of my life (and by extension my body) was about to be challenged, and my old concept of myself smashed and made new. Life was giving the orders now, and I had been effectively rendered dumb. Sitting there, I felt impotent and liberated, at once.

Somewhere deep inside myself I must have already been practising loosening my grip.

*

Every woman holds fears for her forthcoming child, either fleeting or obsessive, and as I am sure you will have guessed by now, I am the obsessive kind.

I spent hours poring over columns of statistics: this pregnancy book offered a 1 in 180 chance of a Down's Syndrome child for a woman my age, that leaflet a 1 in 165 chance. I drove Les mad, asking him whether he thought I should have an invasive test or not, asking him how he thought we would cope if I didn't have a test and we ended up with a Down's baby.

It seemed to me that medical advances of the late twentieth century offer women a double edged sword: never before have women had so many choices, so much help in getting pregnant or avoiding it, so many windows providing illumination into the very building blocks of life, yet never before have women experienced such anxiety, burdened by these same choices. I could now have a test which would provide me with my unborn child's genetic blueprint: the only catch was that I must then decide if I agreed with the master builder's plan. This struck me as a terrible price to pay for new knowledge.

I lay in bed at night tossing up ultimately unanswerable questions, remembering how I used occasionally to accompany my mother to the special schools near Brisbane, where large, smiling teenage boys with incipient moustaches would want to hug me. I remembered little girls with round, flattened faces, rushing up with delight to meet my mother.

I wasn't scared of the reality of an intellectually handicapped child, and some part of me thought I might actually be quite good at being such a child's mother. It seemed to me that I was ready to give and that I would readily accept whatever child was meant for me. At other times my heart fled in panic and grief at the idea of it.

In those first few weeks I read everything I could on every test available, both invasive and non-invasive, and in the end I decided to have the non-invasive tests first. If these indicated there was a problem, I would think about an invasive test then.

At eleven weeks my baby and I underwent the new research test at the Harris Birthright Research Centre at King's College Hospital. Les was with me as the doctor passed the transducer over my belly, trying to pick up sound waves from the tiny human fish swimming below. We watched as these sound waves were translated into images on a screen, and all at once there he was, the entire shape of our unborn child, holding up his arms and waving them about, exactly like a newborn baby.

'Oh, look at him!' I cried out to Les, immediately filled with a conviction that it was a boy, and that he was going to be all right.

'It's a very clear image,' the doctor said, 'they're not always so clear.'

I watched as the doctor continued to do his measurements of this child not yet born, hardly even grown, and suddenly I felt like an intruder. It seemed to me that we were looking into the most private and mysterious home of all and that its owner should be allowed to pass the sacred time between creation and birth alone, beyond eyes. I had such a strong sense of looking into something I should not be looking into that I turned my face away.

'It's all right,' the nurse said kindly, patting my arm. I smiled at her by way of reassurance and turned to watch the doctor, who I knew was looking in particular at the fluid-filled space at the back of the baby's neck, which in Down's Syndrome babies is often increased. As he read out figures, the nurse typed them into a computer which instantly translated them into my personal estimated risk results.

After he had finished, the doctor pressed another instrument up against the fish baby. Suddenly, the room was filled with the swishing noise of the sea which was the swirl of my own blood, followed by the extraordinary sound of another human heart, pumping rapidly as if caught in a net.

Straight away, our baby became vividly alive to me.

The doctor gave us the results immediately: the neck measurement findings indicated that the risk of having a Down's Syndrome baby was lower than my age related risk alone, thereby adjusting the risk to that of a woman aged 35.

'So, that's less than 1%,' I said, looking at the little graph on the right side of the paper he had given us.

'If you want a CVS I can do one while you're here,' the doctor replied.

I wanted to know, but I didn't want to risk my baby. I didn't want to know almost as much, not knowing what I would do if there was something wrong with the baby. More than anything, I did not want the burden of such monstrous decisions.

'It's OK, thanks,' said Les, 'we've decided not to bother.'

We went out into the cold, clutching the test results.

At fourteen weeks we faced the next hurdle, a blood test measuring certain chemicals in the blood which can indicate Down's. The whole process began to feel like one long test, a trying period to be somehow got through, some cosmic exam of our faith, our spirit and nerve.

A friend in Australia was pregnant too, going through the same tests and anxieties as we were. *Fingers crossed for all of us,* I wrote to her, *fingers crossed for you and C and me and Les and all the products of our hearts. I agree with you, all children are 'special', delivered to earth by such tricky and tender means. How can we not love the things we have created out of our own bodies, through love?*

I apologised to her if I sounded over-emotional, but it was because I was. I was all longing and dreams and fears and exhilaration, I was one long swoon of love. I was dreaming our child, that necessary human dream which calls the unborn to us. Later, after Caspar was born and Les and I were fraught and miserable and more tired than we had ever been in our lives, fighting over money and personal space and how we ever got into this mess in the first place, then I would remember how we found ourselves there, how we once lived in a sensual swoon of creation, blind and deaf and dumb to the past and to the future.

All the time I was pregnant I secretly didn't believe my friends with children who told me they had been so tired they were like sleepwalkers in their own lives. I didn't want to know about babies who stopped crying only to gather their breath or two-year-olds who wouldn't let you make a phonecall, pass urine in private or eat a meal without it going cold.

I remember once watching a friend dealing with an insistent toddler who wanted a green lolly, not a red one or a yellow one or any other coloured lolly. 'There are no green ones left!' he ended up shouting, before opening another packet and shoving a green lolly in the kid's screaming mouth. I remember sitting there smugly, self-righteously thinking to myself: 'Children have to learn that life does not always produce green lollies when you want them.' I secretly thought it was all bad management and knew it would be different for me. I could not have imagined that there would be moments when I would willingly stuff a hundred green lollies into a two-year-old's raging mouth in order to buy myself a moment's peace.

I didn't think seriously about such issues as child-care either, or about how I would feel handing my child over to another woman for the day; I didn't plan very much at all. I didn't understand my grandmother when she said: 'The best parents are always the ones who don't have children.'

Like most first-time mothers, I couldn't think beyond the image of which I was dreaming, of holding my own child in my arms.

After yet more nervous waiting, the results came back, giving me a screen negative result for Down's and adjusting my risk to 1 in 630. *A screen negative result does not mean that Down's Syndrome has been completely excluded*, the test report stressed.

Obviously these particular tests did not give a pass or fail, but a figure on a spectrum of risk only, a gambling chip to throw down as we liked. My pregnant friend in Australia described what we were going through as the genetic lottery.

Les and I were tired of living with anxiety. We decided to put our chips away in our back pockets, cross our fingers, and wait.

And what difference would it have made, exactly, if we had known that my friend was to be delivered of a Down's son in the genetic lottery, arriving already loved?

ON DECIDING NOT TO HAVE AMNIOCENTESIS
I saw you moving
in your secret place
a cosmos unmapped,
unbreathed upon.
I am your history
come to claim you
You are my future,

locked.
You are my biggest secret
my hardest lesson
come to instruct me in this:
Going forward
into the dark
is the only way
to capture the day.

January 19, 1995
GREENWICH, LONDON

For the rest of the pregnancy I continued in that dreamy state, calling up the baby we had come to call Caspar, trying to imagine life back in Australia. After several years away we had decided to go home, and it seemed to me that it was not just one new life which was beginning.

As winter turned to spring we took one last trip to Europe. In Italy the trees were already in blossom, and as we drove through Tuscany and Umbria in a rented car an infant sun warmed us. We ate wonderful food and I drank watered red wine; we slept each afternoon.

In Cortona we stayed three nights in a nunnery. When it was time to leave and we were paying the bill the little whiskered nun who was in charge patted my belly tenderly. 'The third one sleeps for free,' she said in Italian.

In Florence on our last night I was lying on the bed before going out to dinner when I felt the baby move for the first time. It was not the soft fluttering I had expected but a definite rearrangement of limbs, and it felt strangely familiar. I had always assumed that the sensation of another living creature inhabiting my body would feel peculiar, even alien, but the extraordinary thing was that it felt natural. It was like something I had long known, as if my body was simply remembering the sensation.

I could have sworn my body carried somewhere within it the memory of creation.

As my belly grew larger I began to experience pain at the top of my ribcage, as if my bones might snap. I did not know how my fixed-up chest with its scar and steel pin would cope with my expanding uterus and one night I dreamed that my scar burst open.

The doctor reassured me that my repaired chest could easily withstand a growing uterus beneath it holding a kicking baby. Privately, I was still not convinced.

The pain was worse at night, and Les laid fresh hot flannels against my skin to ease it. By day the pain quietened to mere discomfort as I sat at my desk overlooking the street, trying to finish a novel about friendship, expatriation and art, set in Hong Kong. I was starting to get panicked about whether I would finish it before the baby came.

Sometimes when I was writing the baby gently knocked against me, like a calf nudging its mother, and I felt ever so slightly annoyed. I felt pinched and ashamed when some part of me protested, 'Not now!' This same part was crying out, 'But the novel!' even as I longed for my baby to come to me. I knew that the baby was greater than any novel I might produce, and yet I still clamoured to write it. I had no way of handling this split in my attention.

Is this a prelude of things to come? I wrote in my red and black notebook. I must have already known the answer.

*

On the first of May I flew back to Australia ahead of Les, who was staying on in order to fulfil various commitments. I had a strong sense that I was taking our child home to his birthplace, where he belonged, where he would fit in with the trees and the rocks and his cousins and grandparents in some hallowed space already cleared for him. In the several weeks before Les arrived in Sydney I found us somewhere to live and began to prepare for our baby's appearance. I registered as a public patient at a hospital and regularly got weighed, had my urine tested and the baby's growth checked. He appeared to be doing well. At last I began to imagine his birth, finally believing he might truly be born to us.

Even though I was only weeks away from delivery, I could not picture what my own, real live baby might look like. My imagination would not stretch as far as picturing us taking our baby home. I went on buying a bassinet and sheets for him, nappies for his imaginary bottom, while all the while some part of me failed to conjure up the reality of a flesh and blood baby inhabiting them.

I see now how impossible it is to imagine your own child before your eyes have seen him. It is like imagining the future, whose outline can only ever be dreamlike, a promise instead of a certainty. Our unborn children are our most beautiful wishes.

Sometimes, walking out of the hospital into the brilliant winter sunshine, I saw people going about their usual business and it struck me as fantastic that the world continued to operate while babies were being invisibly grown in wombs, while men and women were dying and departing for infinity at that very moment.

It seemed to me then that we must necessarily live much of life as if unconscious, for fear of being overwhelmed by the knowledge of how fine the line is between existence and oblivion.

*

Les arrived and scolded me for working too hard, joking that the first sounds the baby would remember would be the soft ping of my printer. In truth I was working like a maniac, racing the baby to the finishing line. Les later blamed part of my subsequent exhaustion on this last bizarre sprint as a childless woman.

Privately, however, I felt Les was underestimating my capacity for work. I had always worked hard and always regarded myself as physically robust, despite my weird bones. If I had to describe myself, I would have said something about being strong and never getting sick, that my body was sturdily built, with well-defined calves and broad shoulders. In pregnancy I had grown fat like a well-tended animal, eating too many sticky date puddings and drinking endless iced chocolates, and when I walked with Les through the streets of Kings Cross and Potts Point where we were living I caused a shiver of revulsion in the gay boys we passed. I was all mother, all fecund, a breathing female animal: my engorged breasts were ready to pump.

Cool, skinny girls dressed in black sipping *caffe latte* on the pavements of Darlinghurst looked away from me. If I was their future, they did not want to know it, and in this way I was rendered invisible. At first I found the experience slightly wounding but quickly felt a giddy sense of freedom: I did not have to wear black or style my hair a certain way, I did not have to keep my face coolly blank or ironic.

Even at my relatively advanced age I was not immune to fashion: up until that moment I had prided myself on at least knowing where the line fell between style and sartorial embarrassment, even if I did not always have the time, money or inclination to dress *à la mode*. Now, I was pregnant and lumbering and completely outside the gates of style and yet I found the experience liberating. For the first time in my life I saw fashion for what it is: a code, a shorthand description, a slightly cruel means of belonging and of excluding. Being as big as a house was strangely comforting: I suddenly understood why some women wear their fat as camouflage.

Les and I regularly walked down to the hospital where we sat in a room with other pregnant couples who were also learning how to give birth. Most were at least ten years younger than us and blessedly innocent of thoughts about Down's babies or indeed anything else going wrong. They sat on the floor like children at a birthday party, each of them wearing an expression of joyful anticipation, as if expecting the most wonderful present.

I remember in one class the teacher discussing various drugs for pain relief (such as pethidine and spinal epidurals) and going on to explain emergency procedures (such as forceps and caesareans). For a moment their smooth collective brows looked puzzled, and after she had finished one young Greek husband roused himself to ask: 'Excuse me, what's the difference between an epidural and a caesarean again?'

Another time I overheard a young man ask the instructor how the baby could breathe in all that water. 'How come it doesn't drown?'

Clearly, to all of us, the creation of human life was at heart fundamentally inexplicable.

Even as the birth day grew ever closer, I continued to be gripped by that lunatic fever to finish the novel. I got up at dawn and wrote well into the night, racing the baby to the ribbon. At times the baby seemed to be sprinting ahead, when a sudden pain gripped me and I thought he was beginning his downward climb, but then the pain would disappear as quickly as it came and I would lie down on the bed for a moment before taking up my position at the desk again.

Instinctively I knew I had to clear the decks, to make both a physical and an emotional space for the baby. I knew I had to have the novel out of the door, as it were, finished and gone from me, so that I would not be pulled in two directions at once. I wanted to be able to devote unreservedly all my time and energy and soul to the baby: I did not want an unfinished novel hanging around my neck.

For me, writing demands complete attention, an emotional stillness, some enormous inner effort of will, intelligence and heart. Instinctively I knew I could not write the novel in my spare moments while the baby slept, as friends had suggested I do instead of running myself into the ground trying to finish it. I sensed that mothering a baby might use up that same will, intelligence and heart required by a novel: I did not want to resent my baby, mourning lost words.

Mercifully, though, the novel was spilling out of me so fast I was having trouble keeping up with it, and one afternoon the last scene appeared to me, perfectly realised.

I stopped what I was writing on a foolscap notebook, and took out the red and black journal in which I quickly scribbled the scene down before it had a chance to escape. My eyes filled with tears as I wrote the last line, and I stood up and went into Les who was resting in the bedroom. I lay beside him and wept. He did not ask what I was crying about.

After that, it was simply a case of joining up the dots: I had the end, now it was only a matter of getting there. I gave up my usual practice of writing the first draft by longhand, and began typing straight into the computer. I had end fever.

On the seventh of August I printed out the last page, and excitedly rushed out to get the manuscript photocopied and bound. I knew I was running out of time, so I arranged for the finished copies to be delivered straight to my much-loved agent and friend Margaret Connolly (who, coincidentally, had delivered a baby girl nine days before).

As if he had waited for me to finish first, Caspar decided that now was the right moment to be born. The very night I handed the finished manuscript over, I went into labour.

The pain woke me, nothing bad, something like period pain and certainly bearable. I remember lying next to Les, on my side with a pillow between my thighs, which was the only way I had been able to get comfortable during the previous few weeks. For some time sleep had eluded me anyway, with either leg cramps or the pain above my ribs waking me, and I had grown used to lying sleepless, breathing quietly in the night.

The flat we were renting was high above the city, and I remember that the curtains had been left partly open so I could see the lights of the buildings blazing like fireworks. Les was deeply asleep and I lay there, not knowing whether the longed-for moment had come, or whether I should wake him.

Minutes later the contractions were more established, although still not really painful. I got up quietly and went into the next room where I had been working, and which now housed the baby's clothes and equipment. I tidied the desk, put a few things away and looked into the baby's empty cot. Even then, it still seemed fantastic that what was happening to me right at that moment would ultimately result in a living body pressing into that very mattress. I didn't know whether to put clean sheets on it.

I was in the bathroom getting my toiletries together when Les peered in, bleary eyed. 'Are you all right?' he asked. I suddenly felt nervous but exhilarated. I felt ready for anything.

'I think it's started,' I said, rushing up and kissing him.

We went into the kitchen and Les started making tea. 'I'd better ring the hospital,' I said. After I had explained to the labour ward sister what was happening ('No, no show; yes, regular contractions') she said, 'Well, you'd better come in then.' All at once I was terrified.

I couldn't drink the tea and I began pacing around the loungeroom while Les rang the taxi company with which we had a prior arrangement. All our pick-up address details were already in a computer and the operator advised us the taxi would be there immediately.

The pains were getting stronger now, and I was bending over the kitchen bench breathing as I had been taught. Les got my bag and we took the lift down to the foyer where, to my relief, the taxi was already waiting.

I remember that delirious drive through the streets of Kings Cross, where hookers were raising their eyes to men and teenagers were swimming in drunken and drugged schools along the footpath. I saw the young boys picking up men in the park near St. Vincent's. I saw lives being lived, even as another life was rushing to join them. I remember moaning just a bit, and the taxi driver not saying a word, not even when he dropped us off at the front door of the hospital. 'Six dollars,' he said, turning around in his seat, not even wishing us good luck.

'He was probably terrified you were going to give birth in his cab,' Les said.

'You'd think he'd have been happy when we got out then,' I replied, slightly shocked at how hard Sydney had become since I last lived there. Then I forgot about the taxi driver and the uninterested eyes of men and concentrated on getting somewhere where I could lie down and escape my own body.

When we got to the labour ward there seemed to be women moaning everywhere, and numerous relatives of Greek or Italian birthing women, drinking tea and eating sandwiches, as if on a picnic.

'You're all coming in tonight,' said the sister who took my details. 'It must be the full moon.'

All at once I wanted to be sick and another nurse rushed me to a bathroom. I didn't know whether it was nerves or the baby but I was shaking and already wondering how much worse the pain was going to get.

'Let's have a look at you,' the nurse said after I had finished, taking me into a room where she helped me up onto a bed. There was a bit of blood now and after she examined me she patted my leg. 'You're already two and a half centimetres dilated,' she said. 'Well done.' I suddenly remembered I needed to get to ten centimetres before the baby could be born: this seemed to me a distance as far away as the moon.

'How do you feel about going to the birth centre?' she asked. 'We haven't got any more beds in the labour ward. Every pregnant woman in Sydney seems to be having her baby tonight.'

I had already decided against the birth centre because I had been told that I was having a big baby (a late scan two weeks before had predicted a possible nine or ten pounder) and because of this there was a possibility of a caesarean. Also, I was unsure about whether I would need drugs and the birth centre discouraged them.

'But she's not supposed to go there, is she?' Les asked.

'I don't care where I go, just get me there,' I said, groaning from the bed.

'We can always transfer her if we need to,' the nurse said, helping me down. 'Do you want a wheelchair?'

'I'd rather walk, thanks,' I said, still conscious enough to remember my manners, for I had not yet fully entered that place between dream and reality, where all the rules are different and where everything the eye lands upon is strange.

I still recognised things around me on that long walk, I remember the paper cup the nurse held under my chin while I vomited again, I remember walking along a glass walkway that seemed to be very high above the ground, with the full moon gleaming and the city standing eerily clear in the night. I remember taking a long time to get there because I needed to stop each time a pain came and wrestle with it till it passed. I felt like a fighter taking it on the chin, I felt like a little girl who had lost her mother. I clung and clung to my darling Les.

In the birth centre the nurse handed me over to a midwife who said she would stay with me till our baby was born. I looked into her face as if she were my saviour and then I dived deep into the sea, the sea of motherhood, of life. I took my place on the lip of my new existence, looked around me for the last time, and dived.

In the sea of pain there were no lifebuoys to save me. I was under, awash, my body was my captain and that part of me I previously recognised as myself, my conscious self with a will, intentions and a plan, was eclipsed. I was reduced (or enlarged) to my true mammal state, my body had freed itself from my authority and was intent on following its own instincts.

In that sea the baby plotted with my body, celebrating mutiny. Together they had already overthrown me, for the baby had filled up my internal dimensions, manhandling organs that had once felt plump and securely placed but now felt squeezed out of existence. My heart had been pushed up towards my throat, my lungs pressed flat, my blood seemed ready to burst from its skin. I sometimes had trouble breathing the air I required to live, as if myself, representing the carrying vessel, was only an abstract necessity in the conveying of precious cargo.

In one moment I understood why labour terrified me: my body

was demanding that my mind relinquish its mastery. I was being forced to acknowledge that my corporeal self had its own plans and would one day make the ultimate involuntary act and expire. Labour is about life but it is also a little lesson in death, a prelude to that other great bodily betrayal. In labour the body's mastery is howlingly unleashed: all your learning, all your mind, all your careful intellectual lessons count for nought. Strokes can fell us, heart attacks, other sudden acts of the body: labour is one such cataclysmic bodily act we can only bow down to, surrendering ourselves up until it is done with us.

In that sea of pain there was only my physical body, the baby who inhabited me struggling to get out and my body doing everything in its power to help him. I was, in essence, a force of nature, howling like the furies, and although I could still see and hear and smell, I was also outside the known world of men. I was mindless as an animal, I was every woman who had ever bowed down before me. I knew all right I was in a warm spa bath in the birthing centre of a hospital: I could even get out when the midwife asked me too. I was conscious as she helped me to the toilet, encouraging me to empty my bladder, yet all the while I was doing these things some faraway part of myself recognised that I had completely lost my former sovereignty.

I rested my head against the cold tile wall when another contraction came and I remember being helped off the toilet and up the hallway to a bedroom where the midwife inserted a catheter to extract the urine I could not pass unaided. 'How much longer, how much longer, how much longer,' I pleaded. 'Get me back to the water.'

Back in the water I still lived in my sea of pain, moaning, moaning, but my new boundless self recognised the shapelessness of water and felt comforted. I tried to remember a baby was coming but the thought kept escaping me and I kept finding only pain to remember, pain to dwell in, pain that was me. It filled me up, to the ends of my fingers, pressing up through the bones of my skull.

'I need an epidural,' I shouted, beginning to scream.

'You're doing fine,' the midwife said, 'you're well along now. Your baby will be here soon.' I had forgotten about the baby: Les passed me a cup with a straw and I bent my head. I was dehydrated; I no longer knew the time, the day, the year. 'Can you stop it now,' I pleaded with Les, whose arms were beginning to shake from the long hours of holding me.

'Do you want to deliver in the water?' the midwife asked, after I found myself squatting, holding on furiously to the taps.

'I can't get out,' I said, 'I can't move.' I was the pain, the water, the earth's elements: I was, of course, at that moment the most powerful woman on earth.

After a twelve hour labour in water, our son Caspar Francis was born at 3.59 pm, on August 8, 1995, a Tuesday wintery afternoon. He was smaller than predicted, weighing 3.6 kilograms, and his delivery was the most potent, *convulsive* act of my life. Just before he emerged from my body he turned around and I felt my internal organs convulse with an enormous energy. I felt the hand of God squeezing the life from me; I was spastic with it, possessed, and then I felt a quietness come and I stopped moaning and started to breathe and Caspar's head came out into the water and with the next push the midwife's hands brought the rest of him up to break the surface.

As soon as I saw him I knew he was mine, the baby I had taken so long to grow up for. I turned around in the bath so I could see Les, shouting, 'He's here, Les, Caspar's here!' The baby was crying and so was I and I think Les was too although he was also laughing.

I could not believe all the joy my arms held, that my arms knew exactly how to hold him. In one stroke I had joined the ordinary world, became a member of the older generation and for the first time felt myself to be an ordinary woman.

I promise you that nothing in my entire life had prepared me for the perfection of his face. Although I did not know then what delivering my child was to cost me, nothing I have lived through since will ever ever take away from me the memory of that sweeping, transcendent moment.

3

A Clock for Caspar

On each eyelid we were carrying a
month of sleep.

CELINE,
JOURNEY TO THE END OF THE
NIGHT

FISTULA n. a narrow passage or duct: an
artificially-made opening (med): a long narrow
pipe-like ulcer (path.): a tube through which the
wine of the eucharist was once sucked from
the chalice.

CHAMBERS 20TH CENTURY
DICTIONARY

After our baby struggled from my body, followed by the placenta which had nourished him, I gingerly walked to a bed elsewhere in the birthing centre. While I lay on the freshly laid sheets believing in miracles, puffed up with pride and what I now regard as a fatal smugness, a midwife who had just come on duty peered into my vagina.

I hardly cared. I remember lying there looking at Caspar in his transparent cot: a fresh soul regarding the room, breathing quietly. It seemed to me that the very air was different and that a kind of gap had opened in the fabric of life, allowing me the briefest glimpse inside. I momentarily felt I understood existence, that long, ceaseless chain of birth and death, and that I had apprehended the workings of love.

Les was standing over Caspar and he too seemed glorious to me. I remembered my friend Suzanne lying in bed after the birth of her first son, thinking to herself: 'I can travel the Amazon. I can love anyone now.' Love was in the tips of my fingers and I only had to lift my hand to sweeten the air with it.

'I don't think I'll do you here,' I heard the new midwife saying and I tried to concentrate on her voice. 'That's quite a tear. You'd be better off in theatre.'

I was not alarmed: practically every woman I know who has given birth has ended up with stitches.

'How many stitches will I need?' I asked, gradually rising to the surface, getting ready to compare my war wounds with my friends.

'It looks like a third degree tear to me,' she said, smiling as she pulled off her gloves, 'I wouldn't bother counting.'

If I could reverse time and go back to that moment I'd rouse myself from my love-soaked dream, call Les to my side, and not let anybody touch me. If I could, I'd stand up and shout for the experts, for every specialist in the country, for the only doctor alive in the world capable of sewing a stitch in the gossamer of an angel's wing.

But of course time, and life, does not work like that. Time, which is the vessel in which life is transported, yields up its secrets as it cares to, beholden to no-one. I was going forward, a passenger in the vessel, and only hindsight has allowed me to recognise the passing of a significant moment.

Indeed, if I had stayed in London would the horrific events which followed never have happened at all? If these are some of the questions I tortured myself with later it was because, in essence, I was still resisting the idea that I was not personally in control of everything.

Which is to say that I was resisting the subversive idea that illness and misfortune and even death are sometimes nothing but random senseless acts which fall upon us without warning.

By the second day, Caspar was gone from me.

A nurse had noticed he was breathing too fast, he was taken elsewhere and it was discovered by X-ray that a tiny section of his lung had failed to inflate. In ninety-nine per cent of cases the lung rights itself, but as a precautionary measure a fine needle was inserted into a vein in his tiny wrist and he was given antibiotics.

As it turned out, Caspar proved to be in the lucky ninety-nine per cent. Nevertheless, the first time I saw him swaddled in his cot in the neonatal ward, amidst bright lights and the blare of voices and radios, my instinct was to wrench the drip from his wrist and save him.

After he was taken it seemed to me that I entered a strange dream. To get to my baby I had to pass through a series of buildings and doors, down darkened corridors and empty, echoing stairwells, and it always seemed to be the middle of the night. I slept an exhausted sleep and each time the phone rang my heart leapt in panic as I was pitched headfirst from slumber.

'Your baby is awake and wants to be fed,' a disembodied voice said in the dark and I placed the telephone back in its cradle, fumbling for the light and my dressing gown.

It seemed to me that I was forever rushing towards Caspar, running through empty buildings, my heart crashing in my chest.

All the while I was literally coming apart at the seams.

One night I dreamt I was newborn myself. I could feel my arms flailing like an infant, my mouth sucking ceaselessly, my new, small body dumb to everything but my own instincts.

How to tell of those first days, those first weeks, when a childless woman invisibly mutates into a mother? How to tell of the process of giving yourself up, of learning to surrender your own breath in order to allow your baby the right air?

A new baby craves nothing less than the whole of its mother, a mother's arms, a mother's body, a mother's milk, a mother's sleep. A new baby takes the sleep from your eyes, the breath from your lungs, a new baby requires that you lay your body down as the bridge on which he will stand.

If I was learning Caspar in those first few days, he had already learnt me. His whole self gravitated towards me as a new bud turns toward heat and light. While I inspected the curve of his eyebrows, the tangle of his lips, he seemed to instinctively recognise me. He always turned his head towards me, towards my breath and my milk, towards the beat of my blood. I was his history, his memory of life and he used me as shelter amid air and light, a safe home away from amniotic water. Occasionally he flung his arms up in what is known as the startle reflex, as if the shock of being in open air was too much for him and he feared falling through space. On the day we walked home from hospital I carried him in my arms in a soft wool blanket and I could not see where I was walking. Every step I took felt precarious. I was holding fresh life in my arms.

At home, my mother had prepared beds for us. The apartment faced west and although it was winter the sun was fierce against the window. I lay naked in clean sheets, trying to sleep between breastfeeds, feeling that I had never before inhabited my own body.

On that first morning home, I remember rolling luxuriously in my own flesh, celebrating my own skin. Every one of my senses was roaringly alive, my breasts had become two live creatures on my chest, my nipples sensitive as antennae. Each time Caspar let out a sound, a small cry or a whimper, my nipples clenched and throbbed, squeezing out a teardrop of milk.

I felt my body had finally been taken up and used, that life had wrenched its way up and out of me. I lay on the bed, drenched in happiness, heat and exhaustion, wanting for nothing.

How to tell of the beauty of Caspar's eyes, like the finest glazed pottery? How to tell of the elegance of his wrists, of holding his head against my breast and feeling hair the texture of duckling down tickling the skin between my thumb and forefinger?

How to tell that his breath smelt of nothing but the purest air, as if he had swallowed a cloud? That the weight of his head in my open palm felt exactly like that of a plump Valencia orange? How each time I fed him I traced anew the outline of his features, learning him like a language or a prayer? I would tell myself I had committed him to memory and then his face would change and I would once again be cradling a stranger.

I was seeing in his face an entire universe.

In those first heady days, before exhaustion and frustration and my sense of outrage that anyone could demand so much from another human being flared into life, I felt only a preternatural calmness. I dwelt in a great ocean of warmth and love, and one morning when Les, Caspar and I took our first trip into the outside world again I felt a wave of pure joy break inside me.

It happened as we were driving our new blue second hand car in the sunshine of a blue Sydney day. As we came over a hill in Dover Heights the sea suddenly appeared, polished and slapping, and I almost shouted out loud with happiness.

I remember that perhaps a second or two later we had to slow down to let some young women cross the road: I looked at their strong, striding bodies as they walked and they struck me as impossibly unused, virginal. They looked somehow *unoccupied*, as if waiting for animation, and all at once I realised that I would never be like that again.

My own body felt ancient in comparison, as if I had been recently torn apart and put back together again: the word that came to me was *rent*. My former body had been torn asunder, my old singular, monolithic self would never again stride out unencumbered.

Yet I felt no grief: I could admire the girls and their youthful bodies without regret, with absolutely no desire to be like that myself again. They appeared like cupboards unstocked, or some great muscle coiled but unable to spring.

I spoke to my friend Emma in Brisbane. 'Did you get a lot of air in your vagina after birth?' I asked. 'I've still got air coming out, it's the weirdest sensation.'

Emma did not remember this sensation. Neither did my mother. Neither did any other woman I spoke to.

Meanwhile, as hour followed hour, I was slowly mutating into a mother. I was turning into a human clock for Caspar, a twenty-four hour instrument of service, measuring out sleep, food, comfort. Caspar Francis, aged two weeks, three weeks, four, had single-handedly overthrown the Gregorian calendar.

My own experience of temporal reality had been eclipsed by his: whenever he opened his eyes in the dark mine opened too, whenever he opened his mouth in request I knew I was the wish he wanted. He pulled me from sleep, from my most private dreams, he took apart my personal body clock and refashioned it.

He lived mainly in a cot by our bed and when I wasn't feeding him I rocked his cradle with one hand to try and get him to sleep. I would rock until my hand slipped in exhaustion and every time he woke again crying to be fed I was sure I had just that minute finished feeding him. In other words, a sense of time had escaped me.

Perhaps because of this, and also because writing things down had always been my way of anchoring myself to the world, I began to note Caspar's feed times. I could never remember when I had last fed him and the lactation consultants and maternal and child welfare nurses and my mother and everybody alive on earth advised me never to feed him more than once every two or three hours. I was supposed to remember which breast he had last fed from, too.

Since I could no longer tell how long a minute was, much less an hour, or whether my right breast felt fuller than my left, I took up my pen. I think now that by keeping my pen and red and black Chinese notebook close at all times I was trying to avoid creative extinction. I think that I was unconsciously gathering in my own personal talismans as a means of pronouncing myself still alive.

In reality, my old self was in its death throes. My pen was recording my last breaths as an unaccompanied woman and my creative self was not facing extinction but learning to write a different book.

Friday, August 25, 1995. Seventeen days old!
12.25 am left breast, 10 mins
2.45 am left breast, 15 mins, burped, asleep 3.20 (wriggling from 3.45)
5.15 am right breast, 20 mins, crying and fighting, tried again 5.45 till 6.15
7.25 am left breast, 15 mins, nappy change, then again 7.55 till 8.45
10.45 am right breast, feed monitored by lactation consultant at the hospital, fought the whole time
1.40 pm left breast, finished at 2.20 pm, settled in cot with difficulty, awoke again at 3.30 pm
4.50 pm right breast, screaming till 6.10 pm
8.10 pm left breast, 10 mins, 8.35 again, 15 mins, settled easily but woke again 10 mins later
11.30 pm right breast, approx. 10–12 mins. (Woke 2.50 am, Wednesday morning)

I longed to witness that singular moment when consciousness bloomed in Caspar's eyes, the moment when he would suddenly recognise the world and myself in it, distinct from him. At the same time I wanted that moment never to happen because I knew this delicious, all-universal, all-timefulness, all-*himfulness* was a once-only, fleeting gloriousness in his life. I knew Caspar *was* the whole world to himself and this time would never come again.

Already I lived with a poignant sense of time slipping away, of something which would not happen twice, which is perhaps another reason why I took up my pen. Caspar seemed sublime to me, irreplaceable, a single act, and I did not want to miss one second of his growing. I still couldn't believe he was mine, that someone wouldn't come into the room and say it had all been a big mistake and take him away. It seemed to me that I had never realised before how bored I had been, how much of my life before Caspar had been a kind of filling in of time. Nothing in my previous life had made me feel so competent, not writing a long and complicated novel, not doing a successful reading or participating in a writer's discussion panel, not lecturing in Amherst, London or Boston. I had a great feeling of achievement.

In those early days with Caspar it felt as if some giant hole in my life I had not known existed before had been filled in. In those early days I had a delicious sense of satiety, as if the want which had driven my life for so long had mysteriously dissolved.

When I looked into Caspar's newborn unseeing eyes I consciously tried not to be too eager to see the glimmer of awareness. I wanted to appreciate fully the 'babyness' of him: I understood that this was Caspar's great moment and his alone, all to do with him and not myself. While I longed to witness his smile, for him to recognise me and confirm me in my role as his mother, I also consciously tried to keep my own self reigned in; I tried to enjoy his blinded grub existence without needing the 'payback' of mirroring.

Once I could not imagine his face. Now I could not imagine the world without him.

It was not until I became a mother myself that I began to understand a mother's power. A mother is the moon and the sun to her infant, a human universe in which a baby dwells. If Caspar could not yet distinguish himself from physical matter, not yet knowing where his own arms and legs stopped and the rest of the world began, he already knew I was both his jailer and his key. It was not until I became a mother that I began to understand my own mother's power over me. I realised that even as an adult I often have to stop and remind myself where my own body stops and hers begins, fearing that if I displease her she may pluck herself from the sky and plunge me into darkness.

My mother has long believed that I have a will of iron and that I always do exactly what I want to do. She could not have known how hard I had to fight to form myself into my own shape distinct from hers, when every instinct told me to cleave fast to her bosom. She could not have known how the mere tone of displeasure in her voice mentally caused me to drop whatever plan I had conceived and take up her plan instead.

Only age and experience and distance from her sun has allowed me to assess whatever advice she gives me, to process it for accuracy and personal fit before I decide to put it on. And yet I know I have absorbed much of what she believes, as plantlife absorbs the sun's rays. A small, childlike part of myself still believes uncritically in everything she tells me.

I used to wonder, for example, if I listened too hard when she told me that childbirth was a breeze compared to doing your first poo afterwards. I remembered something about agony and crying in pain and when it came time for me to do my first poo I squatted cautiously over the cold tile floor of the toilet, a wad of toilet paper in my hand, as if preparing for the slash of the knife.

Was it at that point that I started to unravel? Did my mother's story descend on my head like a prophecy? For a long time I believed that first cautious squat was the beginning of everything, causing the fistula and the rest of the story.

I think now that the doctors were right: the fistula could have been caused by faulty stitching, by being too mobile after a third degree tear (I should have been wheeled to Caspar each time in a wheelchair) or else by the hand of God. In other words, there were a million and no reasons for the fistula.

My belief that I had listened too hard to my mother was a way of looking for a cause. It was also a way of blaming myself for my own stupidity, as if I had personally unpicked the stitches myself.

I will say it again: none of us like to believe in the cruel randomness of existence. Writers, I suggest, more than most. For what is writing but an attempt to trace a shape upon shapelessness, the shake of a tiny human fist at the vast wasteland of the unknown?

But if the rational, intellectual part of myself began to comprehend (and resist) the power of my mother, my body did not. It appeared ready to follow her directives to the hilt.

It seemed that I had always known the story of how my mother breastfed her three children for three months exactly and how each time her milk dried up. With me, the first born, there had been the excitement of a move back to her hometown of Sydney after exile in Brisbane where I had been born.

The story was that the milk just disappeared as she was packing up, and by the time we arrived in Sydney I was three months old and sucking a bottle as if I had been born to it.

When the second baby arrived two years later he guzzled breast-milk as if there were no tomorrow, then vomited it all up and screamed for hours. Apparently the milk dried up for him too, as well as for the third and final baby boy, who arrived eighteen months after the second.

When Caspar was nine weeks old, Les got a job in Melbourne and we began to pack up. In effect Sydney had forced us out: after some ten years of full-time fiction writing I could barely afford the rent on a flat, let alone a deposit on a house. Les had led a life as peripatetic as mine and was hardly rich either, but was certainly more financially secure than me. As well, Sydney felt somehow stale to us, a kind of movie we had seen too many times: Melbourne, where we had never lived, shone like a fresh start.

We packed up our new blue car (which had already blown up once) and took off down the highway. I could feel my breasts emptying of milk as we drove. I felt all my internal rivulets begin to run dry. As if sensing this, Caspar started to cry.

Such is the power of suggestion, such is the power of the body and mind. Above all, such is the power of mothers, whose stories come to us as if from the heavens themselves, mythical, fixed as the stars.

To a woman who longs to keep breastfeeding her baby, breastmilk represents pure evidence. It is evidence of love, of nurture, of the physical skill of the human body to provide everything a newborn child needs to survive. It is a continuation of the symbiotic physical relationship already established in the womb, where the baby needs its mother's body as much as the mother psychically needs the baby to survive.

I had always imagined my body would know how to produce milk and to breastfeed, in the same way it had known how to make love for the first time without lessons. Now I found my ability to feed my child was under threat, and I felt both foolish and enraged, as if my own feet had forgotten how to walk.

Only recently I asked a new mother if she was having any problems with her breastfeeding. 'What do you mean?' she replied with absolutely no idea of what I was talking about. Only a woman who has fought to breastfeed her baby will understand the grief and pain and longing which burns up your veins when the apparently simple act of placing a baby to your breast goes wrong.

I have known women who, rather than give in to the bottle, have worn pouches around their necks filled with expressed breastmilk or formula from which a fine tube runs down to the nipple. The tube is taped to the breast and the baby is supposed to suck milk from the tube as well as the nipple until the breastmilk builds up again.

I have known women with non-existent nipples who undertake special nipple exercises, wearing rubber or silicone shields to draw out their recalcitrant tips. I have known women who have tried to keep on breastfeeding through the fevered agony of mastitis, with nipples so shredded and cracked that the baby mostly drinks blood.

Breastmilk is a living substance, consisting of water, fats and proteins, of living cells like those found in blood. Every half well-read woman knows by now that it is the optimum food for an infant, providing amongst other things growth hormones and cholesterol which help development of the human brain.

Breastmilk is also deeply symbolic. To some women, at least, it represents nothing less than the whole of one's ability to mother.

*

Right from the first my breastfeeding of Caspar was fraught. In our first minutes together in the birthing centre's freshly made bed I instinctively offered him my breast which he accepted, and I naively believed that was all there was to it. I remember crying out at the power of his suck, and my heart surging at the glory of it: I did not know there was a wrong way and a right way to attach a baby to my bosom.

Only later, when my nipples were so blistered and painful that I flinched each time I put him to the breast, did I understand breast-feeding was a skill my body would have to learn. Suddenly I felt as if I had too many arms, or too few, that I had the wrong-shaped hands for holding a warm, perfumed head the size of a Valencia orange.

I had midwives and nurses and lactation consultants coming out my ears, forcing my hand this way, Caspar's mouth that way, aiming him open-mouthed at my nipple like a rattlesnake about to strike. I sat in the special feeding room of the neonatal ward with the other new mothers trying to instruct their own bodies: the air felt hot with our efforts; every woman in the room was intent on the interplay between nipple and mouth.

Like the rest of them I was trying, as they say, to give Caspar 'a good mouthful of breast'. I knew he was devouring me but I tried not to recoil. Instead, I offered myself up, a meal of fresh new mother laid out for his own personal ravishment.

Breastmilk has a vaguely metallic smell, like tin cans. It squirts out from the nipples through a myriad of tiny holes, and the first time I saw this happen I was reminded of a shower rose. A shower of milk into a toothless mouth, a tiny dance of milk upon the tongue.

Caspar was made of milk. He was not yet like me or his father.

His eyes were polished and pure, his milk-fed organs unsullied by anything heavier than water. Sometimes I pushed my whole face into his, into his open mouth, to breathe in the essence of him, his milky ether.

How long did our milky boy lie marooned amongst the noise and the lights before a nurse responded to his cries and called me to him? How long did he lie unnoticed in his transparent cot crying for his mother to save him? Why was he deemed by a passing nurse to be 'a sucky baby' and consequently given a dummy?

I wonder now if that dummy was in his mouth in place of me. I know now that the first days and weeks of establishing breast-feeding are crucial and that it is even harder to bring off successfully if a baby is sick and separated from its mother.

A baby's whole instinct is to feed almost continually, to lie as close as possible to the dull sound of his mother's blood moving, to the regular pump of her heart. Is it any wonder that my body did not rally fully to Caspar's call? That the river of milk intended to be overflowing its banks evaporated into a fine blue trickle?

Oh, I could weep for the loss of those hours. I should have kept Caspar closer, I should have kept him next to me, right under my heart.

In those first weeks in Sydney after Caspar and I came home I clung to our regular visits to the nearby Early Childhood Centre nurse, as if she alone possessed the baby operating instruction manual. I was not confident I could keep him running myself, and it seemed to me that Caspar took one look at Jann and yielded himself up to her strong capable hands like a harvest.

She turned him this way and that, peered into his ears, inspected his bottom, announced that the red rash on his face was not fatal but merely infantile acne. In her hands Caspar did not appear breakable at all but wonderfully, sturdily human.

I was irrationally worried about the bloody looking crust in the folds behind his ears, about cutting his miniature fingernails too close to the quick, about flu-infested people sneezing on him, about inadvertently poisoning him by leaving a spoon in the solution in which his dummy was soaking. The warning label had said not to immerse silver or platinum utensils: could the solution have stripped the metal and consequently poisoned his dummy?

Once I caught one of his fingers in the folds of a jumper I was rolling onto his arm and he screamed as if I had broken it. I put the tiny bone of his finger in my mouth and it was so finely made, so insubstantial, that my giant's teeth could have snapped it clean in two. If Caspar was devouring me, I was also devouring him, for like him I knew no boundaries between us. Intellectually I accepted that I was the adult and he was the infant, yet when a needle pierced his skin, tears sprang up in my eyes.

More rationally, I was worried about the tests Caspar was supposed to have at the hospital because the last scan I had before his birth had revealed that his left kidney was slightly enlarged. The test was supposed to reveal whether any urine was being refluxed back into this kidney, causing the enlargement, or whether it was merely due to a developmental hiccough. If he was suffering from reflux he would need a series of complicated operations.

On the day of the test Caspar was given a needle full of antibiotics before the investigative procedure, and we had to wait twenty minutes for it to flush through his system. I felt upset and guilty, because we had tried to make an informed decision about the continued use of oral antibiotics and decided against it. We had sought advice from early childhood nurses, midwives and medical books, but a specialist at the hospital contemptuously informed us that this was like seeking advice from a hospital cleaner about the NASA space program. Certain doctors do not suffer gladly middle-class know-alls.

In the hospital waiting room there were children with shaved heads and bloated bodies, and a baby only fifteen days old, like Caspar, lying in his capsule with water on the brain and a metal shunt already in his skull.

The baby's mother did not speak at all. His father delivered this information as if against his will, clearly having difficulty believing in the result of an event so joyously awaited. I sat next to the sad father, panicked and uncomfortable in a hard plastic chair, willing myself not to think.

When it was time to enter the procedure room I donned a lead coat heavy as chainmail. I was asked if I could keep Caspar's frail arms pinned above his head while his legs were spread like a frog's and warm antiseptic solution spread over his genitals. A nurse gently placed a green operating garment over him, with a square cut out around his penis, before applying anaesthetising jelly. She then threaded a catheter through his urethra and pumped in some kind of fluid.

Another nurse held a syringe over his penis and dripped warm water onto him in an attempt to get him to pass the fluid back out. Everyone in the room was watching the screen above the operating table to see exactly what happened to the fluid.

I was watching the struggling face of my fifteen-day-old baby, trying unsuccessfully not to cry.

When everything was over, Caspar and his left kidney were

declared to be in perfect working order. That left only follow-up checks on his lungs, and a new knowledge that as long as Caspar was alive in the world I would be forced to consider again and again the black roaring mouth of the abyss.

On the twenty-ninth of August, when Caspar was three weeks old, he smiled at me for the first time. His porcelain blue eyes looked straight into mine, his gaze fixed, all-embracing. I knew straight away it was fully intended and not an inadvertent muscle spasm or 'wind'. Before I knew it I had started to cry, which immediately caused him to stop.

I sat on the bed, weeping, while Caspar continued to gaze at me. I was so tired, I was so happy, I was a complete and utter physical and emotional wreck. I was constipated, my hair was falling out and I did not know why wind was still coming out of my vagina.

All in all I was being given a deluxe, whirlwind tour of life and the only thing I could do was hold on.

The first time the three of us went out visiting as a family I rose from the dining table after lunch and a loud sound like a fart escaped from my vagina. I tried to laugh it off, muttering something about not having complete control over one's body after childbirth, and everyone smiled kindly, and politely spoke of other matters.

I moved with everyone else to the loungeroom but my heart was thumping in panic. I had not even known the fart was coming and, worse, it seemed to have originated in my bottom but emerged unannounced from my vagina.

As soon as I could I rang the Early Childhood nurse, Jann. 'It sounds to me like you might have a fistula,' she said. 'When's your check-up due?'

A fistula. I had never heard the word.

At the six-weekly post-natal check-up Caspar lay in his sling, carefully laid across a couple of chairs, while I spread my legs on a table above him. There was a senior consultant on roster that day, plus a young registrar. 'Have a look at this,' said the junior doctor to the senior consultant, who casually wandered over.

'Oh, I wouldn't be too concerned at this stage,' he said in an off-hand manner to the registrar before addressing me. 'You're off to Melbourne soon, aren't you? They can take another look at you there.'

I remember the young doctor pulling the folds of my vagina apart and insisting the consultant have another look. 'There seems to be something here,' he said, prodding me with a latexed finger.

The consultant pulled off his gloves. 'These things have a way of fixing themselves,' he said to the young doctor as well as me. 'It's far too early to tell if she's got a recto-vaginal fistula.'

I already knew because the Early Childhood Nurse had told me that a recto-vaginal fistula is a minuscule passage running between the two areas. Usually only rectal wind passes through this passage and out the vagina but occasionally there is also what the medical profession calls 'faecal soiling.' That is, microscopic pieces of shit soiling your vagina.

I gathered Caspar up in his sling, thanked the doctors, then walked back to the flat.

In the early hours of the next morning I dreamt that a long, disgusting turd slid out of my vagina.

*

When the cot beside your bed begins to shake you always know your baby is awake. When he is awake he wants only your arms to hold him, only your milk to swallow, only the smell of your breath. You can't open a can of tomatoes any more, or a carton of milk, because you no longer have the use of both arms, and until you work out whether you prefer to live with your baby tied permanently to your body or else with him screaming in his cot because he has fallen from the heaven of your arms, then you can only mourn the passing of your limbs. Your legs, too, have no run left in them because your arms are too full and you cannot lay your burden down to run. You have been stilled by your baby, rooted to the spot, destined for the moment to be a twinned thing, your baby and yourself tied together in a two-legged race. Bizarrely, neither of you is capable of moving.

Once, when Caspar closed his eyes and Les and I laid our exhausted bodies down, I placed Les's head against my breast. I was so used to Caspar it was as if my body did not know any other: Les's skull felt grotesquely huge, like a horse's head in my hands.

Caspar was eight weeks old when it finally occurred to me that for the foreseeable future at least his demands would not cease for a moment. There was never going to be a coming weekend when I could lie in bed all day as if recovering from an all-night party, there was never going to be even one morning when I could sleep in for an hour.

By week eight I had trouble controlling the muscle of my left eyelid. My eyelid kept attempting to fall over my eyeball, as if trying to drown me in sleep. I knew I was awake because I was standing upright but my left eyelid did not appear to agree. I craved sleep in the most intense physical way, as if my whole being was thirsty for it.

Never in my whole life had I known an exhaustion so complete that it seemed to reach the lining of my bones. Every muscle, every fibre, every cell of my body felt used up and exhausted, and each time I woke from a broken sleep my jaw ached from tension. All day along my teeth I carried the residue of clench.

If I had craved to be taken up by life, taken up and out of myself, my wish had been granted. I could not have reached my old self even if I had wanted to because I was underwater, frantically trying to hold Caspar up, pushing hard with my feet in order to get him to air. Down there in the water I did not know which was the deep end and which was the shallow, and could no longer tell which way to start swimming to shore.

When Caspar was seventy days old we raised our waterlogged heads and amazingly, stupidly, full of blind dumb hope and unslept sleep, we took off for Melbourne.

4

The Awful Language

Sweet tears! the awful language, eloquent
Of infinite affection, far too big for words.

POLLOK,
THE COURSE OF TIME

N ow I have to remind you of something.

Since the birth of my sons I always hear things a little later than everybody else: news events, for example, literary gossip. Small children crowd my life, drowning out telephones and television news and radio programs, pushing away newspapers as they make their fierce determined way into my lap. Once I was a voracious reader but now I hardly dare pick up a book.

For instance, I remember how shocked I was when news of the suicide of the American writer Michael Dorris finally reached me several months after everybody else. Dorris was the husband of fellow American writer Louise Erdrich, and together they had three adopted children and three natural daughters. Since one of my most generous friends knows I am writing this book she kindly sends books that might be of interest to me, and Erdrich's *The Blue Jay's Dance: A Birth Year* was one book I successfully managed to finish.

In it, Erdrich writes lyrically of motherhood, joyously unpicking the strands which together weave the whole. In order to protect her daughters' privacy their three babyhoods are refashioned into one, to make up a kind of generic baby-ness. The baby in the book is a nameless 'she' but Erdrich's husband, the father of her children, is always named and proudly declared.

In one section, *In praise of my husband's hair*, Erdrich writes that it was only breathing into Michael's hair, 'glossy and springy ... of an animal vitality and resilience that seems to me so like his personality', that kept her from drowning in the pain of childbirth.

I remember my overriding impression, though, when I finished the book was incomprehension. I could not locate the rage babies inspire in those who love them best, apart from one line about 'the habit of denial and the last secret of female and parental anger is anger against the very object of our most protective love.' Surely it could not be only myself alone who occasionally stifled the impulse to dash my son's head against a rock?

And how did her household work, anyway, with three adopted children (one with developmental delays as a result of Fetal Alcohol Syndrome), and three little girls very close in age, and two adults trying to write and live together? Of course Erdrich quite naturally (and honourably) was trying to protect her family, but at the same time she was also obviously involved in an act of exposure by writing about the intimacies of motherhood and her life.

When the news of Dorris's suicide (and allegations of sexual abuse) reached me it was as if I was hearing news of a close friend. I was shocked because the book had presented a portrait of a composed family, both gentle and strong, rooted through love to the garden of life. The kind of family which made my own in comparison feel unruly, chaotic, governed by infantile rages and impulses.

A few days after the shock of the news began to recede I was left with a strange feeling. It caused me to think about writing anew, about how I sometimes confuse writing with life, how I sometimes uncritically believe that 'truth' can somehow be sniffed down and routed out through an act of courage manifest in writing.

I have already told you that I believed my own writing allowed me to express the unutterable, that my writing *was* myself. Creativity is a land where I run free, but it is also paradoxically the only place where I personally patrol all the boundaries. On hearing the news about Michael Dorris I was reminded again of all the other narratives the story must necessarily leave out in order to build the one 'true' story.

I was forced to acknowledge all over again that writing is *not* life, or even truth, but merely fragments of both, imperfect reflections. There will always be moments and emotions which refuse to be caught, dark undertows which will never break the surface. Life will always exceed the writer's inadequate grasp, no matter how radiant the genius.

Even the master Leo Tolstoy, whom I regard as the world's finest writer, could not catch the whole of life in his net. In his writing net there dwells a vast, overarching compassion for humanity, and a mind whose stretch is so immense it seems to me it must be like the mind of God. Yet Sonia Tolstoy, mother of Tolstoy's many children, told a different story about her husband, revealing the cramped, inaccessible places in his otherwise large and willing heart. Great writing does not equal a great life.

Writing can only ever be a means of refashioning life, sometimes even a way of hiding from it. It can hide all the ugliness and pain behind a satisfyingly smooth surface, all the knots and flaws of existence behind a beautifully fashioned thing called a book which you are now holding in your hands.

I just thought I should remind you of that. Do not place your complete trust in me, will you?

This is the part where I am going to write about rage, about the terrible language of tears. This is the part where I am going to write about the fire which blazed up in our eyes without warning. One day I looked at Les and it was as if we had been scorched, burnt black by the flames. A weird, fierce hatred had been born within us, archaic, demonic. I was the siren woman who had lured him to the rocks, he was the demon lover bent on destroying me.

When Caspar screamed ceaselessly, intolerably, terribly into our ears we turned and screamed at each other. My quiet, gentle Les threw a chair against the wall and I burst into tears of helplessness, rage and exhaustion.

I read somewhere that the result of the arrival of a baby into a relationship can sometimes be like that of a hand grenade tossed in the door.

Caspar exploded in our faces, blowing up the known world.

This is how the body reacts when a baby keeps screaming and screaming: the heart of the mother begins to pound harder, thrashing about in its cage of bones, squirting out blood. The temples throb and the spit on your tongue and between your teeth dries up. Sweat springs up in the palms of your hands and the soles of your feet, and every instinct in your body tells you to escape; but you cannot run. You will hear screams in the shower and in your dreams, you will hear screams through walls and through deepest sleep, you will hear screams through the very lining of your head. Your whole body will be one long scream and here is the rub: there is nothing you can do to stop it.

If you have already tried picking up the screaming baby, tried giving him the breast, tried rocking him in comfort, tried showing him his own screaming face in the mirror, tried putting him on the floor, tried putting him in his pram, tried everything in short that you can think of, your only chance is to close the door and leave the room at once.

Go out into the garden and take long, loping strides so that your feet touch the earth and you remember again that you are a grown woman alive in a rented flat in Tennyson Street, Elwood, Melbourne, Australia, The World, The Universe, and that screaming, wailing, monstrous creature on the pillow inside is your very own infant son.

In Melbourne it was supposed to be spring, but the air and the sky still lingered in winter. We took out our jumpers and kept the heaters on and while Les went out to his new job I attempted to sniff out my new territory. But it was always Caspar's sleep time or else once outside the front door he wouldn't feed and we had to come straight home again. More often than not, I was simply too tired to get up from my chair.

I never seemed to get much further than the park at the end of the street once I did stand up, although sometimes I triumphed and managed to reach the giddy heights of the Acland Street shops. It felt as though some giant hand was pressing down hard upon my head, keeping me underwater. I was not just housebound, I was drowning in my own life and only through a great effort of will could I push the great hand off and make a rush for the surface.

Melbourne might just as well have been the lost city of Atlantis, so remote and inaccessible was it to me. I remember driving through its centre one night with Les, Caspar screaming in his capsule in the back, my breasts hard as rocks with unshed milk because he refused to feed from them. The city appeared like a film set, fairy lights twinkling in the trees, with grand, corporate buildings representative of the public world of men. I saw a sophisticated man in an expensive suit come out of one of the buildings, and he looked sealed off, safe, remote as a distant planet from the reek and roar of earthly existence.

I thought: no wonder men are scared of us. We are all milk and guts and blood, the very jaws of life, a constant and bloody reminder of the beginning and, thus, the end.

One cold afternoon during the wolfing hour, that time of late afternoon and early evening when a baby's sensory faculties get overloaded and he erupts like a screaming kettle, I wrapped Caspar in a rug and placed him against a pillow at the far end of the sofa.

I sat at the other end, watching him. I suppose I was waiting for him to open his mouth, but he surprised me by sitting silently where I had placed him. He looked strangely willing, so unprotected, so *unwrapped* sitting there, that I was shot through with a wrenching painful love.

All at once I had a shocking new awareness of Caspar as a separate human being, an emotionally sentient being with his own charter, his own needs and wants. After the intense concentration on his physical wellbeing — the constant nappy changes, the rocking to sleep, the bathing, the massages with baby oil, the rubbing of the crack behind his ears with sorbelene, the feeding, the feeding — I suddenly understood that he was also a creature of human emotions.

A feeling like embarrassment or shyness overcame me. It seemed to me that I was being introduced to a person I did not know, another person with a private interior world unavailable to my inspection. At that same moment Caspar's personality seemed to arise from its baby fug and it struck me that the tiny human person sitting across from me might be described as peaceable, sensitive, reflective, self-possessed. He seemed to have a sense of humour too, to be friendly and interested in what was going on around him. In other words, he was a separate and complete other person with an entire human personality inside him.

Instantly I was flooded by a sense of my own inadequacies, that this new person would see them and unmask me as the fraudulent mother I was. I was suddenly convinced that I would be inadequate for the task ahead, of leading Caspar single-handedly into the waters of life, of being both his compass and his light. I did not feel honourable enough, or cut from the right moral cloth, and all my failings suddenly appeared too large.

It took all my courage to lean across the sofa and pick him up. 'How do you do,' I said, holding him up beneath the arms and speaking into his face. 'I'm very pleased to meet you, Mr Webb.'

He looked back at me in all his perfection, still unmarked by the fingerprints of life, not yet ruined by a single mistake or regret. He was his own blank canvas and it was absolutely clear to me that it was not myself who was holding the brush.

Before we left Sydney, Les and I had attended one of those sessions run by Mothercraft nurses who perform miraculous displays of settling babies previously unknown to sleep. Before your very eyes they take the most atrocious screamers and instantly stun them into sleep using only their bare hands.

The one we had was young and pretty and childless and infants fell back from her gaze as if hypnotised. She patted them hard on the bottom and *sshhhed* loudly into their ears and within minutes they fell into comas. Consequently, every mother in the room felt the utter uselessness of her own hands.

She gave us tips on how to rock their cots, how to reduce visual stimulation by covering their prams and bassinets when you were trying to get them to sleep, how to swaddle them so they felt safe, how to massage them after a feed.

She told us: 'There is no mileage in feeding a tired baby' and 'If you can get them through the first hour they usually sleep after that.'

Les even took notes in my special book. I see now that he wrote, 'Look for tired signs' and, most amusingly, 'Stay relaxed.'

This is as realistic as telling the driver of a small car watching a ten tonne truck coming straight towards her to stay calm. I was as capable of staying relaxed as that driver. And anyone reading this who thinks that a comparison between one small human infant and a ten tonne truck is ludicrous obviously has not been personally confronted by the sheer force of an infant's lungs at full blast.

I am here to tell you that if the lungs do not give out at the moment when you think they should, indeed if they go on and on and on until you fear they will go on for the rest of eternity, then jackhammers, dentists' drills, sirens, terrible music, incessant car alarms, the full cacophony of modern life combined, is but the mere twittering of birds.

I am here to tell you there were moments when I would have preferred a ten tonne truck to squash me flat so that I did not have to listen to that sound for one second longer.

One morning in a park with Caspar screaming in a sling around Les's neck, Les screamed at me that he was not an endless, bottomless pit in which to dump all my anxieties. He yelled at me that I was overly anxious about Caspar being cold, anxious about him being too hot, anxious about finding him dead one morning from Sudden Infant Death Syndrome. I was anxious about Caspar's lungs, anxious about his kidneys even though I had been assured they were fine, I was anxious about every single fucking thing.

Everything he said was completely true. I burst into terrible tears.

Sunday, November 12, 1995: Notes I've been meaning to take for some time — 1. Wrapping Caspar up, Les says he curls up like an echidna or a porcupine. He curls himself into a ball — legs and arms drawn up towards his chest, burrowing down with his head. He's a total delight.
2. Sometimes when I'm so completely exhausted that I can hardly keep my eyes open, irrational thoughts go through my head. This morning, in that second before I was properly

*awake, it occurred to me that I hadn't heard Caspar stirring
yet and I thought: 'If he's dead, at least I'll be able to sleep.'*

Several things had come out of our session with the Mothercraft
nurse who performed miracles, not all of them good I believe now.
For example, either Les or I spent hours rocking Caspar to sleep,
not even bothering to take him out of his pram. It was one of those
giant Emmaljunga things with a bassinet fitting, designed to look
like an old-fashioned English nanny's pram (and very fashionable in
Melbourne I discovered where we had bought a cheap one second-
hand). We rocked and rocked, pushing Caspar back and forth, back
and forth over the carpet. We rocked him when we were half asleep,
when our eyes were falling out of our heads, we rocked him till our
arms ached and we had to change hands. Once when I was angry
because he never seemed to go to bloody sleep I rocked him so hard
that the pram flew from my hands and would have crashed into the
wall if I had not stopped it.

Now, whenever we pushed the pram out of the house and into
open air, Caspar greeted the world dressed in a kind of baby
chador. We kept him almost permanently draped in an ongoing
effort to get him to sleep: we draped his pram, we draped his
bassinet, we draped his car capsule (both inside and outside of the
car). We kept him tightly swaddled, too, in rugs, and always seemed
to be endlessly wrapping and rewrapping him. I wondered if it was
apparent to the rest of the world that I was a little anxious.

Whenever I saw other babies in their prams with their free limbs
sprawled in what looked to me like a kind of ecstasy I felt a pang of
envy for their mothers. Whenever I saw a mother casually remove a
fat veined breast from her shirt to feed her child in broad daylight,
I resented both the woman and my son.

In order to keep breastfeeding Caspar, in order to persevere with the idea that he must continue to keep suckling my milk at all costs, I had to remove myself to a quiet, darkened room with no distractions, sometimes draping a cloth over both him and my shoulder to ensure he could not see a thing except my hopeful breast.

Even then he sometimes screamed and refused to feed. 'Put him on the bottle,' advised my mother. 'Forget all this earth mother bullshit and reclaim your body,' advised a friend. 'He's not putting on enough weight, why don't you try one supplementary bottle a day?' suggested the maternal and child health nurse.

Like the best Resistance soldier I was determined to fight till the end.

In Melbourne I quickly found a new maternal and child health nurse to act as my guide and saviour. I had a baby book too, because books had always told me about life and I did not see why a baby book should not instruct me in the same way. It had quickly grown tattered and dog-eared, like the bibles of certain lunatics, because, like them, I also looked towards my book for salvation. (And, like any proselytising lunatic, I will tell you the name of my bible: *Baby Love: Everything you need to know about your new baby* by Robin Barker.)

On my very first visit to the new baby nurse I sought advice about the fistula. Because I know you will want to know but are too polite to ask, I will tell you that Les and I had already successfully had sex without any ill effects. I was full of trepidation beforehand, but I did not split in two as I had feared and indeed as far as I could tell the fistula did not make any appreciable difference.

The baby nurse referred me to a good local female doctor who then referred me to one of Melbourne's best female obstetrician and gynaecologists.

In the doctor's waiting room I looked through a photograph album of her successful deliveries. I was already more interested in what the album left out.

'You've most certainly got a recto-vaginal fistula, dear,' pronounced the doctor after she had examined me, 'and very poor pelvic floor tone, which can't be helping the rectal wind.' I liked her but was interested to note that she used the same epithet a male counterpart might, and that her manner towards me seemed authoritative and distant, with a hint of dismissal.

Fear passed through me and I suddenly understood why doctors must learn to construct a self-protective wall to live behind in order to avoid a deluge of human emotion.

'What are the implications of having a fistula? Can't it just be re-stitched?'

She sat forward in her chair, scribbling notes on a patient card. 'And you haven't suffered any faecal soiling?'

I swallowed. 'No. Might I in the future?'

'The only time you might is if you get a bit of diarrhoea. You musn't panic if it happens, it's just that watery faeces passes through the fistula more easily.' She looked at me. 'There's no real urgency about doing a repair and I would advise that you leave it until you've finished breastfeeding, until your vagina is oestrogenised again. You'll get a better repair.'

She stood up and walked me briskly to the door. 'Enjoy your baby, dear, breastfeed him as long as you want to, then come back and see me when you're ready. We'll talk about a repair then.' She gave me a wide encouraging smile and, amazingly, I was briefly comforted.

*

Here is the part where I learnt to hide in humour, because humour kept me safe. Humour kept the dogs of fear from snapping at my heels, from chewing at my ears, from spitting foul matter in my face. Nurses use black humour when confronted by the bodies of children; living soldiers have been known to shake the dead hands of their mates. I took up humour as my cudgel too and shook it hard in the dog's face.

I made cynical, desperate jokes to my friends about the serendipity of finding a publicity angle as obnoxious as Will Self's heroin flirtation, more shocking than Linda Jaivin's views on younger men as sex partners: *Australia's only writer capable of farting out her vagina!*

This is the part where I learnt to hide under cover of motherhood. In seeking refuge from that which was too awful to contemplate, I discovered one of motherhood's oldest secrets: that infants offer a place to hide, a human skin not your own in which to retreat. Infants can single-handedly obscure outward reality, by acting as a kind of human roadblock to every outstanding problem and uncertainty in your life. In this way they keep fear at bay by placing their small bodies directly in your line of vision, blocking out everything else.

You will not have time to think about fistulas, or even consider anymore the larger question of who you are, because your 'self' as you once knew it has gone missing in service to your baby. Your self, that once struggled to shape itself into your best true self, to find its way to the best life, to the best book, to the blazing self you knew must be out there somewhere, that 'self' is no longer.

You will not agonise any longer about whether you chose the right career, about being passed over for jobs, even, for the moment, how to get back in. The world of public life is unavailable to you: your whole existence is mapped in the bones of your baby's face.

I once knew in passing a woman who had borne six children and now I knew why. As each baby assumed childlike dimensions she would once again find herself pregnant: I understood now that she did not want to emerge from that bath of oblivion, that drowned existence from where the world of public life appears inconsequential, foolishly self-important. In that bath of forgetting the cares of the world are nothing but a long-ago dream.

Once, a new friend asked me if I had experienced any difficulty relating to my sons after all the damage I had suffered in giving birth to them (and she didn't know about the colostomy). Since my sons were the waters in which I dwelt, the boundaries of my world, her question had no resonance for me. My sons to me were simply everything: water, life-raft, retreat.

Les and I were fighting over money, although I know that actual money is rarely the real issue. Money simply stood for us as a receptacle for all the fury, resentment and frustration that had sprung up between us. Les felt trapped, for he felt that he had returned to the same situation he had been in twenty years before, with his first dependent wife and two sons. He felt as if all the years of hard work in London had come to nought, angry that I had somehow misrepresented my financial position and that I seemed bent on continuing to write even though it meant impecuniousness for us as a family. I felt that he was asking me to give up my life's work, out of some stunted notion of equity: if he was not doing what he wanted, why should I?

Les had intended a different kind of life for himself back in Australia — part-time work, more time to do the things he enjoyed. I would scream back that he knew I was a writer when he married me and I had never represented myself as wealthy. What did he want me to do, give up my work, just so he could work part-time?

We always ended up shouting at each other, with me feeling that my deepest self was under threat. It was clear that each of us felt stranded in misery. What was at the heart of our pain was the large matter of self-fulfilment versus duty towards others. In essence, each of us wished to know what we could ethically claim for ourselves in this new structure of family we were creating.

My good friend Sandra believes that having children is the best cure known for egomaniacs of the Me Generation. If Les and I had long been used to helping ourselves to whatever we wanted from life's table, now we couldn't even reach up to tug on the edges of the tablecloth.

One morning I saw advertised in *The Age* a well-paying job for a creative writing teacher at a Melbourne university. In the stressed, hare-brained manner in which I now conducted my life, I somehow managed to send off a CV between breastfeeds. In due course I was offered an interview.

The morning of the interview I scheduled a breastfeed for Caspar just before I left the flat, hoping he wouldn't require another feed before I got home. Because I didn't know where I was in Melbourne whenever I was removed from the streets I had marked out as my territory, I left early in our dangerously unpredictable blue car, the street directory on the passenger seat beside me.

When I finally arrived my hands were slick with sweat. I still couldn't keep the muscle of my left eyelid from drooping, and before I got out of the car I blinked several times as if to blink away unslept sleep.

In the reception area I asked if I could make a quick phonecall to check on my baby. 'He's fine,' Les said, 'good luck.' It was the first time I had re-entered the public world, and I felt like a child in a world of grown-ups. Standing in the reception area, just moments before I was due to go in, my confidence entirely deserted me. I tried to tell myself that I was an adult woman, a mother no less, a real writer published in Australia, England, America and France. None of it made any difference.

When the door to the interview room was held open for me, I stifled the impulse to turn on my heels and run away. Only deeply ingrained social propriety made me offer up my sweating hand, which I had just managed to wipe.

Inside the room was an interview panel, made up of the dean of the department, two lecturers and a young man from Personnel. Every thought in my head fled at the sight of them.

I will spare you the details of my mortification, but I will tell you this: the world of public life and a newly hatched, breastfeeding mother are not meant for each other. A baby will not fit in between the cracks of life, and I was being given a demonstration to prove it.

After that, I knew for sure that I would have to invent a new way of being alive, encompassing not only myself now but Les and Caspar too, a caravan of souls, moving together.

Caspar was still not acquiring the weight expected of him on the baby growth chart. 'It's genetic,' said Les, 'he's like me.' It was true that Caspar might have sprung fully formed from Les's body, so little did he resemble myself. A small part of me was disappointed, even disconcerted by this. Caspar was nothing like me or even anyone in my family, and there were moments when he seemed like a visitor. At these moments I found it hard to recognise him as my own, or indeed as anything to do with me, and yet his very unfamiliarity also allowed me to see him as his own separate person.

Like Les he was long and thin and, eerily, when they were head to head their heads were identically shaped. Caspar's ears were tiny replicas of Les's, his neck a genetic echo. I wondered about the millions and millions of genes which had collided to form him, the remnants of grandparents and long dead uncles caught in his bones. I marvelled again at the myriad of connections which life had miraculously got right.

He still cried a lot and still fought at my breast. Sometimes he barely put on one hundred grams in two or three weeks when he was supposed to be putting on a hundred per week. The child health nurse suggested that if I still didn't want to offer a supplementary bottle of formula, I should try expressing between feeds to stimulate and thus increase my milk.

Whenever I think back on this time, it seems to me that I was constantly on the phone when I was not attending to Caspar. I was always talking to the health nurse, or the after hours maternal and child health telephone service, I was always talking to someone from the Nursing Mothers Association about various ways to fend off the bottle.

Les got cross and told me I was stupid to be taking any notice of baby growth charts anyway because it was obvious to anyone with any sense that not every human being could fit into a statistical curve. 'He's just skinny,' he insisted and I would have believed him except that I was not confident enough to shout down the voices of authority telling me Caspar was not thriving. I was too frightened of inadvertently killing him.

So I learnt to use a plastic device designed to draw milk from my breast. At the kitchen table I placed my nipple in a rubber flange and tried to work out how to pull the outer plastic cylinder up and down so that it worked as a kind of suction pump. My hand ached from endless pumping, from waiting for what is known as 'let down', that sweet tingling moment when milk bursts forth from the nipple.

I pumped fruitlessly at the table for minutes, for half hours at a time, mostly yielding only twenty or thirty millilitres when the milk finally did flow (to make up a bottle I needed anything from 120 to 180 millilitres). I began getting up in the middle of the night when my breasts were fullest, to try to catch the milk unawares, so to speak.

I was piling tiredness upon tiredness, left wondering how long I could go on.

Tuesday?
12.45 am rb 15 mins, lb 15 mins
2.45 am lb 15 mins
5.10 am rb 15 mins, lb 15 mins, in bed with us, squirming
6.50 am lb 5 mins, back in bassinet
7.10 am rb, 5 mins, back in bed with us
Bath
9ish, lb, 10 mins (asleep 9.30 till 10 am)
10.50 am lb 10 mins
12.20 am rb 7 mins
1.20 pm lb, 15 mins, rb 5 mins (asleep 15 mins)
3.55 pm rb 5 mins
4.40 pm lb 15 mins
6.45 pm till 7.15 pm rb, 20 mins, lb 15 mins
10.30 pm lb 20 mins, rb, nibble only
3 am Wednesday, rb, 15 mins (awake 4 till 4.45)

When Caspar rejected my milk, my arms, my proffered comfort, I understood him to be rejecting my very self. For I had long believed that a mother is given the gifts with which to comfort her child, to quell his tears and to launch him into his bed of dreams. When Caspar repulsed me, I felt angrier and more deeply rejected than ever before.

WHY IS IT SO HARD? WHY WON'T YOU DO WHAT I ASK? WHY WON'T YOU GO TO SLEEP WHEN I LAY YOU DOWN, WHEN MY BODY IS SO EXHAUSTED I CAN'T RAISE MYSELF FROM THE BED? WHY WON'T YOU STOP IT? STOP IT STOP IT STOP IT I'M DOING EVERYTHING I CAN EVERYTHING I KNOW I'M USING EVERY SINGLE PART OF MYSELF DOING THE BEST I CAN TRYING MY HARDEST GIVING YOU MY WHOLE LIFE AND STILL YOU WILL NOT CO-OPERATE WILL NOT SIMPLY LIE YOURSELF DOWN AND CLOSE YOUR EYES. WHAT DO YOU WANT FROM ME? WHERE DO YOU COME FROM, WHERE TIME AND SPACE AND ENERGY MEAN NOTHING TO YOU?

Here is what I had to find out for myself: all my life I had believed that if I put enough effort into something, enough will and dedication and energy, then I could achieve a successful outcome. When Caspar exploded into my life I was forced to put aside forever any notions of effort equalling outcome. I had to teach myself to expect nothing, to let whatever situation he and I were in to reach its own conclusion.

Caspar was my ultimate Zen test.

Each small milestone of a baby's life is acknowledged by a mother not only as an occasion for celebration but also as a means of counting the steps back into her own life. A first tooth represents one step, the first meal of solids another, the first night a baby sleeps alone in a separate room a third.

When Caspar was just over three months old, we decided to move him into his own room. As I closed the door on him, child of my womb who had lived within me and next to me for so long that I no longer remembered the world without him, I felt the catch of grief in my throat. I recognised that an irreplaceable part of our life together was over and I felt a great wish to push open the door and gather him up. At the same time I knew that I would have to let go. As I walked away from the door with tears in my eyes, a bloom of relief burst open in my blood. I realised that the closed door also represented a small victory in the war for my freedom, a small step on the road back to myself.

As soon as I thought this, a rancid guilt engulfed the bloom.

On Caspar's one hundredth day of life I went to the Queen Elizabeth Centre to have his feeds monitored. He was still not gaining weight and I was clearly drooping from exhaustion: the health nurse had advised me to go as soon as possible. It was one of those centres with both a day clinic and rooming facilities where exhausted mothers and their sleepless or colicky or breast-refusing babies retreat for rest and advice.

Emma's husband Kevin (who has also become a dear friend) refers to them as Distressed Mothers' Homes, and I felt myself to be a complete and utter failure to be going to one. My mother the sun, a superb organiser herself, had led me to believe by her example that not being able to manage a baby was indicative of failure of character. Consequently, even though several of my friends had got their sanity back by admitting themselves, I had always secretly thought it shameful not being able to cope with an itsy-bitsy baby. (Motherhood is a great lesson in humility.)

At the centre they let me rest while they tried to put Caspar to sleep. On a flowered couch in another room I was so strung out I could not close my eyes. When it came for the test weighing of Caspar before and after a feed I was not surprised to learn my flaccid breasts had only provided him with less than half the milk a baby of his age required.

The midwives advised me to book myself in for the next available room. 'You need to have a rest and we'll have to work out a way of getting this little fellow to put on weight and learn to sleep properly.' I felt as if someone had offered me a fortnight in the Bahamas, and couldn't wait to get home and pack.

Several days later Caspar and I were comfortably ensconced in a tastefully decorated room with our own bathroom and a double bed for visiting fathers. 'Luxury,' said Les, putting on a Monty Python voice as I showed him around. 'Oh, before I forget, someone from Picador rang.'

He handed me a piece of paper with a name and telephone number written on it. It was my publisher, and when I called her she was anxious to know when I could begin editing the novel I had completed the night I went into labour.

I was about to find out just how realistic my recent vow to invent a new way of existing was. That is to say, my old life and my new were about to meet head on.

5

Milk and Ink

A woman must have five hundred pounds a year
and a room with a lock on the door if she is to
write fiction.

VIRGINIA WOOLF
A ROOM OF ONE'S OWN

'With the birth of each child,
you lose two novels.'

CANDIA McWILLIAM

This is how I learnt to become a writer: I dug deep into the earth of my own life until I struck bone. Then I dug deeper and deeper still, until I dug my way out again into other lives not mine. I listened hard to the lives of my friends and family, to passing strangers on a bus, I taught myself to watch closely and to read the spaces between words and lines. I learnt to take what I saw and what I knew best and wrest it into some kind of shape recognisable to others. The stories I built were constructed from my tears, my yearnings, my joys and deepest imaginings and in this sense they exist as a version of myself. The tumbling innocent boy from *A Big Life* comes straight from my yearning for a kind of transcendence, the lost Rachel and the drowning Anne-Louise from *Hungry Ghosts* come from that place inside myself where grief and love dwell.

I have already told you that before I learnt how to do this trick I was floundering. My life was a kind of soup of experiences, with bits floating here, chunks floating there, a brew of chaos. Learning how to take these disparate experiences and form them into an intelligible whole gave me my first sense of control over my own life. It seemed to me that when I finally completed my first novel at the age of twenty-nine I also completed myself, assuming at last the defining outline of the person I was meant to be.

From that moment on I had no doubt that I would be a writer for the rest of my life. I was burning up with a million ideas, each lighting fires in my blood: I wanted to write about the loves and despairs of families, about the difficulties and ecstasies between men and women, about the lost middle-aged, middle-class men I once met while researching a newspaper story about an Indian sect and the anguished bewilderment I witnessed in their faces. I am embarrassed to admit that I wanted nothing less than to write about how it felt to be alive at the end of the twentieth century.

I saw myself too as a kind of witness to lives which would otherwise be lost, to lives which would otherwise go unrecorded. At that swooping moment when I finished that first novel, I believed my sole purpose on earth was to write the best and truest book I knew. I was in a fever to begin and nothing was going to stop me, not even my own waking life. In my waking life I forgot to eat, I refused to answer the phone, I got angry with friends who had a day off work and dropped around uninvited because they knew I'd be home. Indeed, my waking life, the life in which I had a physical body needing food and water, friends and lovers who needed to be fed, that waking life sometimes struck me as an inconvenience, existing only to get in the way of my pen.

If I was only rarely articulate in my waking life, suffering *esprit d'escalier* at every crucial point, in my writing life all the right words were at my disposal. I had wit, charm, courage, strength of character, even coherent thought patterns: in short, everything I needed. In my waking life I cared too much for other people's good opinion of me, I occasionally lacked courage, my thoughts were frequently scattered. In my waking life my arguments were often wandering and inept and my actions somehow more cowardly and less high-minded than I intended, but in my writing life I was totally fearless and everything cloudy was magically rendered transparent. I was intoxicated by writing, completely in love, not the first writer to prefer life in a book to life in the physical world with my eyes open.

I will tell you a secret: a waking life is not enough for a writer. I needed a kind of parallel life to soothe me, to speak for me, to make darkness visible.

It obviously took me a while to learn how to serve up the soup of my life so it was edible. When I was nineteen, twenty, twenty-one, I took flying leaps at writing but always landed back in the soup where I had started. By the time I was twenty-five I was getting closer, having learnt that I had to first ignite the fire under the pot. It wasn't enough simply to stir the ingredients, unexpected herbs had to be added, exotic chillies, the temperature had to be right. I found out by experimenting how to tease the tastebuds, how to titillate the saliva glands. I learnt, in short, what to throw out and what to put in, how to keep the stomach hungry for more.

You want to know what happened about the fistula, don't you?

Like all novels, the novel I finished the night I went into labour sprang from the marrow of my bones. *Hungry Ghosts*, a story about art, friendship, betrayal and expatriation, set in Hong Kong, came directly from my experience of life. In my waking life I have been both betrayed and the betrayer, I have lost friendships and lived in Hong Kong, certain friends have occasionally happened upon the same boyfriend as myself and I also know intimately the relationship that art bears to life. I took what I knew and refashioned them into a new story.

All writers can only write about what they know. In my case, because what I write is sometimes close to the outward facts of my life, the books I construct are often read as straight autobiography. I am here to tell you that I can indeed be found in my books and it might even be argued that my deepest, unconscious self lives within them, inaccessible to my waking eyes. Yet every book is also a construct, a product of a working imagination, and as such every book is a lie impersonating a truth.

Certain readers have tried to track down (or claim to be) the originals of my characters. I am sorry to have to tell you that you will never find the source of the spring, for I have taken from this person here and that person there, ransacked my own imagination and robbed from the most shameful or most celebrated parts of my own nature. Certainly some characters more than others are more obviously aspects of myself, standing as my representative in a story, but no character I have ever written fully describes my complete waking self. My complete waking self is, like your own and like Walt Whitman's and like everybody else who has ever been born, as 'dazzling and tremendous as the sun', and as such, is too hot and too large to fully apprehend.

I am also sorry to be the one to tell you that even though I might have taken aspects of your character, your manic laugh for example, or your poignant willingness to hope against hope, you will not stand as your complete waking self in the refashioned story either. For I have taken your head and repositioned it on someone else's body, I have taken the most vivid characteristics of your personality and blithely grafted them on to someone else entirely.

I have to admit though that I have stolen from you. I steal shamelessly from my family and friends, from the faces of people in trains, I steal from my lovers and husbands. I am a writer and my job is to steal life in order to paradoxically amplify and magnify life, my job is to at least attempt to reveal life to you in finer, more astonishing detail than you have ever before seen it.

I am a writer and, as Graham Greene once admitted, all writers have in them a chip of ice. Certainly I will do my best to act honourably, to be as gentle as I can, but I have to warn you that I am also life's witness and if I need to use a hair of your head to give life to my character, I will not hesitate to pluck it.

To supplement my income (let's be honest, to *provide* an income) I occasionally teach creative writing classes. I can always tell the real writers from the would-be writers: the would-be writers agonise over the question of whether people will be hurt by what they will write. 'What will my mother think?' they cry, chewing their pens. Here is the answer: a real writer has no mother, no father, no lover, no friend, the moment she takes up her pen. A real writer undergoes a kind of moral amnesia when she is writing, in which her actual life is split off from her writing life as if by an axe. In writing, your only moral duty is to your characters, to the lie you are creating which must, in the end, burn more radiantly than the truth.

By now you are probably getting some idea of the unswerving zeal which goes into my writing, of the almost religious intensity required when writing a book. Whenever I was writing a long complicated novel I lived in the grip of a kind of lunacy, a manic solipsism which blocked out everything but the book in my head.

By now you are probably getting some idea too of why I took so long to make up my mind about whether or not to have a child, for the question of whether motherhood and writing were mutually exclusive was a very real one for me. I wanted to write the best book I knew but I also wanted to learn to live more fully and richly in the world. I wanted a life in which I wouldn't crave that other parallel life more. I did not wish to die having lived a safe life in the pages of books, I wanted to dash my tremendous sun against someone else's dazzling sun, risking even pain and destruction.

In my old writing life, telephones could remain unanswered, friends could be turned away at the door and impatient lovers sweet-talked into waiting until Friday to go out. In my new writing life Caspar shone the entire force of his light in my eyes and refused to let me look away.

Male writers with limited incomes and partners and infants are often burdened by the need to earn more money. Their writing often goes out the window for a time while they take a 'proper' job, but very often once the baby is no longer a baby their partner returns to full or part-time work, leaving the writer free to write again.

For a female writer with a limited income and a partner unhappy being in the breadwinner's box, the options are fewer. A female writer has a different relationship to her child than a male writer too (no matter how shared the parenting) and is often less able to claim for herself the right to write at all. A woman's dedication to her craft is sometimes seen as less valid than a man's, able somehow to be shifted to one side when other people's needs intrude. Throughout history male writers (and artists in general) have had wives and lovers and daughters willing to act as midwives at the birth of art, but most female writers have birthed books alone, having relinquished entirely the idea of giving birth to children.

There in that Distressed Mothers' Home I placed my birthed child on my shoulder while I spoke on the telephone for the first time to the woman who was going to edit my novel. My birthed child was squirming and I found it difficult concentrating on what the editor had to say. I can't remember if I asked her whether she had a child or not but I meant to.

The world was a different place to me now, you see. One morning it struck me that Caspar would die one day, not soon, not while I was still alive I hoped, not until he was a very, very old man. But one day he would no longer exist and for the first time in my life I fully understood what it meant to love someone beyond life itself.

*

The first night in the Distressed Mothers' Home Caspar was put in a cot in a tiny room across the hallway from me and I was told not to bother getting up if he cried. 'We'll look after him tonight. You have a good sleep.' I showered and put on an unglamorous nightie (with buttons down the front so Caspar could get to my breasts) and then I went to bed.

In the darkness I closed my eyes and tried to sink into the deliciousness of long-awaited sleep. I had dreamed of sleep while standing with my eyes open, pushing Caspar's pram back and forth, back and forth. I had physically yearned for it, as if desiring a lover to come into me. I had prized a night of unbroken sleep more than world peace or permanent happiness and now, after more than one hundred nights of broken dreams, sleep would not come to me.

I lay in the darkness with my ears pricked like a dog's. I listened to the muffled cries of babies in their holding pens, of two-year-olds separated from their mothers for the first time, of newborn twin boys wailing for their bottles. I listened to each and every cry, trying to identify Caspar's, knowing every nuance of it, every pitch, every pause. I could not hear it.

When I was convinced he was dead, I got up. On the pretence of asking for a sleeping pill, I crept across to his door and quietly opened it. By the soft light of the corridor I saw that he was sleeping peacefully, his arms flung out, his generous lips caught in their usual tangle.

I shut the door and walked to the nurses station where I asked for a sleeping pill which would not pass through breastmilk. 'They all do, but we've found these are the best. They're very gentle,' the nurse said as she opened a cupboard and took out a bottle. She rolled into her hand a small green pill.

I swallowed it and went back to my room. I resisted looking in on Caspar again and climbed straight back into bed. I closed my eyes and before I knew it I sank into an exhausted sleep from which I spontaneously awoke at dawn.

As I opened my eyes I heard Caspar crying to be fed. Immediately I felt my breasts to find out if they had magically filled with milk in the night.

That same morning, Caspar tasted milk other than mine. I watched him struggling with a training cup, drinking the milk which was recently white powder inside a can, and it looked all wrong. It looked somehow dangerous, an act of insurrection, and I felt the rise of bitter, bitter tears. Oh, why couldn't my own breasts have spoken more eloquently, calling him with the right words? Why didn't they work the way they were supposed to work, filling as soon as they were emptied?

Both the Nursing Mothers' Association and my baby bible advised a training cup rather than a bottle, for milk from a bottle flows into a baby's mouth faster than milk from a breast, and once a baby understands this he often opts entirely for the bottle. You can see how determined I was to keep breastfeeding, can't you? It was only fear that Caspar was starving to death that made me prise open that first tin can.

That morning I watched him at his training cup, swearing not to cry, swearing not to let my own ego get in the way of his hungry stomach, of his growing body, of his own sweet forming ego and that terrible but certain day when he would walk away from me for good.

In a second conversation with the editor (this time without Caspar on my shoulder) I was able to understand more clearly her ideas for editing the novel. Perhaps because I had written *Hungry Ghosts* in such a white heat, pressed on by Caspar's imminent arrival, I recognised that I would have more re-writing to do on this novel than I had on any other. Usually when I submitted a manuscript to a publisher it was pretty clean and I did not have to touch it much, other than doing a line edit for more obvious mistakes of grammar or facts.

This time I needed to do a lot of work, defining more clearly that character there, illuminating motive here. I would have to go through the whole 350-odd page manuscript as if completing another final draft.

Shit, I said aloud once I was back in my room.

I had no family at all in Melbourne, no loving Nana to mind the baby while I wrote my book, no sister with babies of her own. I hardly knew anyone, either, and my one friend in the whole of the city, Tracey Callander, had two small children herself and was recovering from a severe bout of post-natal depression. Obviously I couldn't burden her.

I asked the other women in the Distressed Mothers' Home if they knew of any reliable but inexpensive nanny service. I felt Caspar was too young at four months to go to a day-care centre (he was still being breastfed, just).

The mother of the two-year-old laughed. She was a children's clothes designer who was attempting to be both a mother and to do her other job. 'Welcome to the merry world of child-care,' she said, rooting around in her bag for her address book.

On New Year's Day, 1996, when Caspar was about to turn five months old, I began work on the editing of *Hungry Ghosts*. I sat at the kitchen table, wearing ear plugs while I concentrated on the screen of my portable computer, trying to pretend that Caspar wasn't behind me being entertained by Carol on a rug on the floor.

Earlier, when I had rung the nanny service, I had been asked whether I wanted a nanny who attended to the baby only, or one who would perform 'light household duties' such as a bit of shopping, light cleaning, cooking and so forth, but who came at a slightly higher rate.

Since I was hard pushed remembering to put out the dirty nappies for the nappy service we had recently acquired (having decided that financial hardship was preferable to the work and time put into washing nappies), I opted for the 'slightly higher rate'. Within months, any money I had already earned in advances was completely gone.

It was hard to work at the kitchen table that morning because Caspar's muffled sounds somehow still wormed their way into my ear canal, I had to stop work and feed him regularly, and Carol was apologetic but she often had to interrupt me to ask where something was or if Caspar preferred his cow's milk on his cereal biscuit warm or cold. Sometimes she couldn't help passing into my line of vision and the thought I had been trying to track down escaped entirely while I gazed at the back of her head. She didn't know either the magic rituals I used to get him to sleep, so private and particular were they, as they are to each mother and baby. I had to show her.

It was hard to work at the kitchen table because Caspar's warm breath was in easy reach, his skin would be warm if I touched it. It was hard to work because Caspar kept getting in the way, poking his human hands and eyes into the fabric of my imagination, jostling the characters caught in its weave.

The characters put up a good fight though, and there were

moments when I longed for my son to be taken far, far away. Whenever Carol took him to the shops or for a walk my old self returned and I blazed through words like a flame. I had to learn to be fast, faster than I had ever been, for every second counts with a child. I had to teach myself to commit phrases and words to memory when I did not have a pen, to scribble notes to myself on the backs of envelopes or VicRoads car registration notices. I learnt to compose everything in my head rather than on the page, to have whole paragraphs, whole chapters, completely worked out before I even sat down. Much of this book has been written in the same way. I write this book in dreams, in buses, in the quiet moments before I go to sleep, in the ink of my blood. I have learnt to write in air now.

Back in the Home, before Caspar and I were released, the nurses and lactation consultants were convinced that all I needed was a decent rest for my milk to come gushing back. In my baby bible, too, rest was advocated: a few days of doing nothing but lying around feeding the baby, drinking cups of tea and reading books. Since I was writing a book and not reading one, the only thing I could do was try to get as much rest as possible between furious bouts with words at the kitchen table.

As soon as Les got home in the evenings and Carol had left (she was proving to be so gloriously tireless that I had to practically order her to take a break) I took off all my clothes and filled the bath. The bath was actually a spa, no longer working, and when it was filled it passed for a small pool. In the spa I tried either to empty my head of thoughts or else drift off into a kind of meditation in which I imagined my breasts to be full of the creamiest milk. I was not sure if New Age affirmations worked but I was willing to try.

Most of the time my neck was so full of tension that whatever position I was in quickly grew uncomfortable. I felt as if my whole body was being squeezed in a vice: my heart felt ready to burst, my head pounded with trapped blood. The deadline for the delivery of the manuscript was fast approaching and I still had chapters and chapters to go. I knew if I didn't make the deadline the book couldn't be published when it was scheduled to be and the publishers would be very cross indeed. I wondered if they would ask for the advance money back, and what I would do if they did because I had no money left to give back.

In the bath I told myself to relax. *Relax*, I willed myself, once again feeling the familiar residue of clench along my jaw. I had only been out of the Home for a matter of weeks, and already felt as if I had never been. I was no longer sleeping at night, knowing even as I lay rigid and despairing in the bed that it was the worst thing I could be doing, that I needed all the sleep I could get, for my milk production, for my sanity, for Les. The harder I tried to sleep, the more my body lay as if flayed upon the bed, skinned of dreams.

Les was feeling completely marginalised, squeezed into my life between Caspar and the book, a poor third. 'Just give up the fucking book!' he shouted one night and I shouted back, 'I would if I could!'

The terrible truth was that the book drew me, I compulsively craved to perfect it, I longed to write the perfect last line and could not have given it up for anything.

But Caspar also drew me and I wanted nothing less than to sink forever below the surface and never write a book again. I did not want to ruin the once-in-a-lifetime experience of Caspar's first months of life, to lose what milk I had left over the stress of writing a book which would only end up on some suburban remainder table anyway.

And Les drew me, the shimmering memory of our joined flesh and all our lost happiness I still felt might be found. I was caught in a bloody crossfire between milk and ink and love, and could not have borne any one of them to be vanquished. I felt as if I was being forced to choose, as if my own hand was holding the gun.

I should admit to you now, lest you have the impression that I toiled on alone in my duties to Caspar as if I were a single mother, that from the first Les was deeply involved in Caspar's life. In the earliest, darkest days, when Caspar seemed to do nothing but scream, Les walked him endlessly round the streets of Darlinghurst and Potts Point and Kings Cross, dodging vomiting girls and winning syrupy smiles from spaced-out prostitutes. Les took his bath with Caspar every night, changed as many nappies as me when he was not at work, grew to know and love him as intimately as myself.

Sometimes I even felt the clutch of jealousy when Les soothed him when I could not, when I recognised one morning that the two of them shared some wordless, intuitive language. From the first Caspar's and Les's personalities were complementary, and it was evident that Caspar was more like him than me. They were both quiet, self-possessed, highly sensitive, independent. Caspar often pushed me away with a tiny fist when he felt me to be in his face, as it were, and my personality was sometimes too excitable for his taste. Occasionally when I shouted too loudly in pointing something out to him he literally jumped, his mouth crumpling. 'Oh, darling,' I crooned, comforting him, 'I was just showing you the helicopter.'

Once I was feeding him in his bouncer in the kitchen while Les was reading. 'Do you have to babble on to him all the time?' Les called. 'Can't you be quiet for once?' From the look on Caspar's face I would have to say that Caspar clearly agreed with him.

Have I mentioned before the struggle babies make of everything? Their struggle to sleep, to ease the pain in their bellies, their furious struggle toward poise, co-ordination, ease? They strain their whole bodies, every inch of their whole inchoate selves towards some instinctive notion of a cohesive, fluid self.

When Caspar discovered his own hands at the end of his arms it was a revelation. For days, weeks, until he discovered his miraculous toes, he held each hand up in front of his eyes, turning them this way and that. His hands obviously struck him as wondrous found things, for each time he saw them again it was as if they were newly discovered. He turned them delicately, deliberately, as if admiring the changing light on a beautiful ring on his finger. He never tired of looking at them.

Not long after he discovered his toes, Caspar rolled over for the first time and not long after that he began the enormous struggle to sit up. He was struggling to form himself, you see, to control his own limbs, at the beginning of the dance of himself. He was learning his own dimensions.

One day in January when Carol was playing with Caspar on the floor where I could see him from the corner of my eye, he pushed himself up into a sitting position and stayed there. I jumped up from the table, pulling out my earplugs as I ran, and knelt down in front of him. 'You clever boy!' I said, remembering to speak quietly. He had seen the earplugs in my hand however and, in reaching over for them, he promptly fell over.

*

Have I told you yet of what I regard as a baby's greatest trick? How a single baby obliterates both the past and the future, insisting only on the present, on Here, Now? Already with Caspar I had forgotten the long, hourly wait for him, my lumbering pregnant hugeness, my difficulty in breathing at night. Already I could not remember exactly the feeling of pain above my ribcage, of feeling as though I was going to be pregnant forever, or of standing under the shower watching my stomach rolling as if it contained a bag of puppies. I could not remember precisely the terror of believing the baby would never come, that weighted, immobile feeling when I could not remember not being pregnant, like I was some great rock evolved over centuries, timeless. I can only tell you of these things because I wrote them down.

Now, I couldn't have told you what Caspar was like when he was born, nor even what he was like a month ago, and I certainly couldn't see his daily growing. I noticed of course when he did something new, when he noticed his fingers for example, but I couldn't see exactly how one day, by delivering him into the next, was growing him. At four months, at five, he was still more like an atmosphere to me, surrounding me, inside me, like air, like a personal climate. I still existed as if only for him, dragged from my own life, as if all points of the earth converged on him. He was Here and Now, the very essence of time itself, experienced as both stasis and motion. I *knew* time was moving, understood Caspar to be moving in it, yet I felt stranded in Nowness.

But if Caspar had wiped out the past, he had also wiped out the future: his very Nowness prevented me from imagining him with a full set of teeth, standing upright. Like the time when I couldn't imagine his face, I now couldn't imagine him speaking, crawling, walking. Once, my father-in-law asked me what I hoped Caspar would be when he grew up: it was as if I had been asked to imagine Caspar as a seven foot African. I couldn't picture Caspar beyond his six o'clock bath.

This is what mothers speak of when their eyes get that soft glow and they say with nostalgia, *They're only little for such a short time.* In this sweet, short time, the past and the future do not exist, there is no such thing as loss, as bitter, dashed hope, and not one single promise has gone unfulfilled. In this sweet, short time, every bad act is as yet undone and there is only the never-ending, glorious present, these blameless limbs, unwrapped, like a gift.

At the end of January, the book still unfinished, the lease on our temporary furnished flat was due to expire and Carol was about to start another full-time job. The thought of house-hunting in the midst of book-writing and full baby duties with no Carol paralysed me. Apparently everyone in the whole world but us knew that there are some things you *never* do around the time of a baby's birth: move house, renovate your old house or get a new job among them. We had done most things you weren't supposed to do, plus move countries as well.

But, in a wonderful play of irony and serendipity, a young woman I had met through the local Baby Health Centre, years younger than myself but nevertheless worn out by caring for a sleepless baby with no family support, decided to return to her native South Africa with her Australian partner. Their beautiful two bedroom flat with a study in St Kilda was soon to be vacant.

I rushed around to the estate agents as fast as my little feet would carry me. I filled out an application form and after a few days of nail-biting, we were told the flat was ours.

Just before we moved in, a telephone call came from the removal firm arranging the delivery of our furniture and goods from London. 'When do you want it delivered, love?'

By early February I was standing in the lounge room of the new flat. Caspar was crying and he still wasn't sleeping at night, so my left eyelid was still closing of its own accord. I still had what is known as a diminished milk supply, the book was still unfinished and there were thirty-eight large boxes, twelve small boxes and several large containers of paintings and prints to unpack.

I wondered if there was some way I could shut my eyes and vanish.

If in the early weeks of Caspar's life I had felt myself to be drowning, now I felt myself tangled in a net. I was nearer the surface of the water now but floundering and fighting, getting more and more twisted up in the tangled skeins of my own life.

Every evening I tried to unpack yet another box before Caspar woke up again. I was still writing as fast as I could and I had another nanny now, less willing than Carol, who had already balked at the concept of going out to get a loaf of bread. I had finally been forced to ring the nanny agency to clarify the term 'light household duties'.

'You've got more crap than anyone I've ever known,' said Les, as I unpacked the boxes, which were mostly mine. I am the kind of person who hoards everything: every letter I have ever been sent, old identification documents, I even found one of my old boyfriend's former girlfriend's old Australian Journalists Association membership cards. I have pamphlets from Women's Liberation House in Brisbane, school essays, leaflets from the feminist abortion referral agency where I once worked in 1979, even copies of my own letters.

In ways that I cannot fully explain, I think the hoarding is akin to my writing. I am chock-a-block with memories, stuffed full of unruly life: I do not want even the smallest thing to pass out of existence without being acknowledged and saluted.

Summer finally arrived, just as it was about to be officially declared over. The flat was light and airy, with an upstairs and a down, and after Caspar went to bed we sometimes dragged the kitchen chairs outside. We drank a glass of wine each and felt as if we had drunk ten, for parenthood had made our lives both smaller and larger. Already we were no longer used to going out into the world with large appetites; it was as if our pleasures had grown refined: less was more, one single glass of wine went straight to our heads.

When I stared up at the sky above Caspar's bedroom, my small life felt fathomless as the moon. My head was full of wine, my heart full of thanks and I was writing a poem to Caspar in the air. *You are my France*, I wrote.

I'm still writing it.

On top of everything else, summer also brought to life a plague of fleas which had been hibernating in the carpet. One afternoon I went to put Caspar in his cot and found dozens of black spots jumping on the sheets.

I stripped them and called out to the new nanny, who was downstairs. 'Would you be able to bring the bucket and mop up please? There are fleas up here!' We had already found one or two on Caspar's legs from the carpet downstairs, but I had thought the polished boards in the bedrooms upstairs were safe.

The new nanny came upstairs with the bucket and mop. 'Here you are,' she said, handing them straight to me. My arms were full of squirming baby, bedsheets and jumping fleas. 'I am not employed to scrub floors,' she announced, her cheeks flaring.

I could have strangled her.

Amazingly, against all odds, I finished the book. One day, the moment I had longed for finally arrived and I reached the last line. I never wanted to read a word of it again.

I jumped up from my chair and did a small dance of joy around the room, feeling a great rush of release. I ran downstairs and scooped Caspar up from the rug, swinging him around in my arms in the loungeroom. The nanny came in from the kitchen, an unsteady smile on her face. 'I've finished!' I cried, 'Yippee! Hip, hip, hooray!!' At that precise moment I did not care if I never wrote again, for I had loathed the whole tortuous process. I had clearly not succeeded in seamlessly blending my writing life with my life as a mother and a lover, yet neither had I pulled the trigger on the gun. I realised that from now on my life would always be more tangled, more complicated, heavier to lift. Yet I also felt that in the process of finishing the book I had somehow expanded, as if I had swelled in my own skin. I felt as if I had added to the sum of my parts.

'Mummy's finished her book, Cappy! I've finished!' Caspar was smiling and smiling, letting out delighted squeals while I twirled him around and around. Book, apple, car, monkey: it was all the same to Caspar. My big serious adult life meant nothing to him, all he knew was the twirling and twirling, me, his laughing, newly released mother, holding him up in her arms.

Perhaps by now, all these years later, you might even have found that book of my personal war washed up on some remainder table or library shelf. Inside its pages you may be able to detect tears, the scent of milk, a baby's howling. You may feel the flame of my life race up your fingers and know a little of what it feels like to feel burned.

For in its pages my actual waking life smoulders still, giving off the kind of smoke which always lingers in the wake of an incendiary blaze.

Reader, can you smell it? Can you?

6

Wild Reality

Sleep hath its own
world,
And a wide realm of wild reality.

BYRON,
THE DREAM

According to every sleep scientist of the late twentieth century, when Caspar entered his sixth month of life he had magically reached the psychological stage when he could be taught to sleep through the night.

In babies younger than six months the circadian rhythms which tie the pattern of our lives to a twenty-four clock are not yet fully operational. In other words, those biological reminder bells which gently tell us when we are sleepy, when it is time to wake up, time to get hungry or time to eat do not ring loudly enough in a baby. A very young baby cannot distinguish himself from the air, let alone tell the difference between night and day. He also needs to be fed frequently.

As well as all this, certain forms of adult sleep are completely absent in a newborn baby. Those forms require a particular sort of brain maturation, and newborns require huge amounts of REM (Rapid Eye Movement sleep, where the body and brain are at their most active) which is believed to help this maturation process.

In other words, before the age of six months a baby cannot be taught to sleep through the night because he hasn't got the brains for it.

But when a human baby reaches the magical halfway point in his first year on earth, every sleep scientist alive considers him grown enough to be pulled from the waters where he has lived until now, oblivious as a fish. It seems that Caspar's own clever body had delivered him to this terrible moment, for apparently even in the womb he was practising his breathing during REM sleep; his brain was growing big enough to receive sensory input so that he could see and hear everything even before he was born to the air.

Now, delivered up to this moment on a sheet in a white cot with his eyes wide open, Caspar was going to learn to close his eyes and keep them closed for nine or ten hours at a stretch, never opening them once.

He was going to learn how to go to sleep without a dummy in his mouth, without being rocked into his dreams, without his mother or his father standing fixed by his side, immutable as the stars.

In the second half of his first year of life Caspar was going to have to learn how to do without everything he had lived by in the first half. Everything we had used to get him to sleep until now, all the advice we had been given about rocking, the use of a dummy, the singing of lullabies, the reduction of visual stimulation, every single prop we had ever used had to go.

Here is the sleep science behind controlled crying, that baby cognitive therapy program designed to teach a six-month-old baby's brain a new sleep pattern: if a baby is put to sleep by rocking, by feeding, by falling asleep in your arms, by any external aid whatsoever other than by his own devices, then later in the night when he enters the light sleep phase all humans pass through, instead of coming up nearer to the surface and successfully passing back into deeper sleep again he will wake up.

You see, when he is closer to the surface he senses that his mother is not there, that the dummy has left his mouth, that the milky breast is elsewhere. His external aids, everything he associates with the act of passing back into sleep, are absent and thus he cannot get himself back to sleep.

In controlled crying, also called more gently and euphemistically 'comfort settling', the idea is that the baby teaches himself how to get back to sleep. He is permitted a comforting suck of his own thumb, a favourite toy or blanket, but it is now up to him to teach his own brain the logic of sleep.

The 'controlled crying' part means that you do not leave a baby abandoned in his cot crying his heart out the whole night, but go in at regular intervals to comfort him. You are not allowed to pick him up, rock him back to sleep or do anything other than comfort him as briefly as possible before leaving the room. You leave it a little longer each time before you go back to comfort him, so that the baby learns to wait: he knows you will come back and that he is not abandoned forever, yet he also knows that when you come back it will hardly be worth it.

This is the theory. According to the books, by the second or third night (sometimes after only one night!) your baby will have taught himself how to sleep through the night. Certainly there will be some crying, perhaps two or three hours of crying, perhaps even a vomit or two. Tell your neighbours that you are teaching your baby to sleep so that they won't think you are murdering him. Be kind to your partner, maybe even stay up all night together drinking tea and eating chocolate to make things easier. Whatever you do, work together as a *team*.

I never thought I would turn into the type of mother who practised such barbarity. I never thought I was the kind of woman capable of listening to the anguished cries of a baby who cannot understand what is happening to him and cannot know why I do not rush back into the room to save him. Hadn't I always come immediately the moment he cried?

Before I gave birth to Caspar I was the kind of woman who fervently agreed with a friend who on any night had at least one or two children in her bed and who believed that letting babies cry broke their spirit. Before I had Caspar I didn't think it remarkable in any way that a child shared the marital bed till the age of five, or six, or seven. I believed a mother offered up her days and her nights, her very life to her children as the food which grew them. Certainly she didn't leave a baby abandoned in his cot.

After I had Caspar and my left eyelid continued to hang over my eyeball as if I had suffered a stroke, after I grew so tired that I became physically clumsy and cut my fingers on knives and suffered a black eye walking into a door after stumbling out of bed for the fifth time in a single night, after I started to suffer dangerous lapses of attention in my daily care of Caspar (letting him roll off the change table and catching him just in time or failing to strap him properly into his stroller and thus failing to stop him from falling out onto his head), after all this I thought I might possibly have turned into the type of woman who might consider controlled crying.

After one hundred and eighty-five nights of waking three, four and five times a night I considered myself conquered.

Before the fateful night's arrival, I went to the mother and baby group at the local Baby Health Centre. I had not been since the young mother whose flat we had taken had gone back to South Africa. Now I had finished the book I was eager to learn Melbourne, to overlay upon its features my own personal map.

Sitting on a rug on the floor, our babies lying on their stomachs or crawling around our knees, I asked the other women if any of them had done controlled crying yet. Two women immediately concentrated on their babies, busying themselves with extracting the torn pages of a book, wiping a chin, while the most outspoken woman looked at me askance. 'I wouldn't dream of it!' she said. 'A baby's a baby. Where's it written that they're supposed to sleep through the night? I think controlled crying's unbelievably cruel. God knows what it does to their psyches.'

I looked down at Caspar on the rug, trying to crawl on his

stomach, propelling himself by his elbows like a soldier in under-growth. 'Is Rose still sleeping with you?' asked another mother quickly, subtly shifting the territory.

'Yes,' said the outspoken woman, 'I feed her about twice during the night. She obviously still needs it.'

'A friend of mine's got this great idea to encourage her little boy to sleep in his own bed. He's been sleeping with them since he was born and he's four now.' I looked up at the woman speaking, the kind one who had changed the subject and was obviously still trying to avert an argument. My hands were sweating. 'She's got this chart pinned up behind his door and every time he sleeps in his own bed he gets a gold star. He's really proud of himself. She says it's working really well.'

The outspoken woman smiled at her. 'Oh, what a lovely mother!'

As for me, unlovely mother with sweaty hands and a heart plan-ning on abandoning my own son to his cruel crying fate, I did not speak again but hung my conquered head in misery and shame.

I'm sorry, baby, I'm sorry. I just thought that if your own mother killed you by inadvertently dropping you on your head, you would never forgive me. I just thought that if I couldn't do my mothering properly, that is, fully awake with all my five senses working, you may as well not have had a mother.

I just thought that by delivering you up to that terrible moment I was giving you back a fully functioning mother and thus helping you as well as myself. I was helping you, I was helping Les, I was helping all of us, wasn't I?

At least that's what I told myself. At least that's what I told myself as you cried pitifully on and on, as I found you trembling uncon-trollably in your cot, your tiny arms flailing wildly, your whole body one enormous sob. At least that's what I told myself as I ran from your room, my breasts crying milk, as Les and I screamed at each other as we failed to work together as a team, as I dug my fingernails into my palms or held the pillow down over my ears to try and muffle the sound when I fled to my bed.

I was going against every single instinct in my body. Every single instinct I possessed was telling me to leap out of bed and scoop you up in my arms. Every single instinct I possessed was telling me that I was your mother and my duty was to save you.

I wasn't allowed.

7
The Full Cup

My cup runneth over.

PSALMS,
XXIII, 5

C aspar survived his ordeal, without becoming autistic or even emotionally scarred (as far as I could tell), and after two nights he started sleeping peacefully all night. I felt as if the whole world had turned happy.

He began to sleep more soundly and more predictably during the day, too, noticeably enjoying himself more when he was awake. Now, every morning when I awoke the sun was shining, flowers bloomed, happiness romped in my heart.

It seemed to me that my energy returned and my limbs once again reached their full stretch. Each day assumed a satisfyingly calm and predictable shape, with clear blocks of time when Caspar slept, when he played in the warm autumn sun on the floor, when Les and I dared to consider our future.

A project I had taken on in the last months of my pregnancy (editing a short story collection called *WomenLoveSex*) was coming together effortlessly, with some good stories coming in as the deadline approached. The project did not seem at all unmanageable and indeed it seemed to me that beneath the autumn days I could sense the shape of my life again. The days were no longer falling over each other like endless waves in a vast, unnavigable sea.

We started to venture out on little jaunts in our blue car, to the Dandenong mountains, to the beaches around Sorrento. The car was still unpredictable, in truth a piece of junk and a bad mistake, but nonetheless Caspar now sat happily upright in his new seat in the back, capable of pointing out with his finger anything which took his interest.

In the warm autumn days we explored Melbourne's parks and began to think about the possibility of buying a house. We were both nearing forty and we had lived until now impulsive, peripatetic lives. I was sometimes gripped by anxiety about my perilous financial position, wondering if the price I had paid in choosing to write books was too high. I had once had a part-share in a house, for example, but had been forced to sell it in order to finance my writing. I sometimes wondered if it had been worth it.

For every Peter Carey there were hundreds of writers like me, ecstatic to sell 8,000 copies of a book. I knew all the stories about writers far greater than myself who had manuscripts rejected and wrote on regardless, but the effect my own modest book sales had on me was to make me doubt whether my instincts as a writer were right. I had taught writing students who could not rub two words together yet they could not be budged from belief in their calling and I sometimes wondered if I was any different to them.

In the warm autumn days, as I approached forty, I began to assess my life. I knew I wanted a house, somewhere where I wasn't at the mercy of rising rents and the whim of landlords. I wasn't sure anymore I could go on living as I had before, whether I could go on writing always worrying about money and how to pay the next bill. I felt I had lost my nerve.

In the warm autumn days Les and I talked about our lives, about whether having children was essentially a conservative act. Certainly having children most often means you are obliged to stay in one place, to establish some kind of solid edifice from where a child ventures forth. Having children most often means you cannot get blind drunk, leave town, run off to join the circus.

Here's what I think: until you have children you can often exist without having to act on your deepest beliefs. Once you have children all your most hidden rules rise to the surface like cream. You will know then if your trendy, inner-city existence is just a coat you put on or whether it is in fact your own skin. You will know if you cannot bear to let your child's head go unbaptised that you have not abandoned your faith as completely as you once thought. You will know if you cannot send your child to the rough local school and

wish him to go to the same private school you once loathed that you
are more bourgeois than you ever suspected.

Having children exposes you. I will know who you are when I see
how you wish your children to live.

Les and I were beginning to understand the enormity of our position, to feel the wind of exposure.

While the sun was still shining, my parents came down from
Brisbane. They were staying in a motel not far away and planned
on hiring a car for a few days. They knew Les had to work, but
wondered if Caspar and I would like a few days away.

Les was happy for us but Caspar only gazed mournfully at his
father, refusing to wave while we drove away. Caspar's smiles were
hard won and consequently much prized. 'He's a serious young
chap, isn't he?' said my father, turning around in his seat. Caspar
looked back at his grandfather, unsmiling.

'You were the same,' said my mother. 'Serious as a judge. You'd
look at everyone with a baleful expression. You looked like you'd
been here before.'

In the back of the car, nearly forty years old, I was finally learning
how to smile. I thought: *it's really true. Having your own child
means you finally understand your parents' hopes and fears for you,
makes you capable of seeing their full glorious frail human selves.* I
suddenly understood that their intentions towards me, towards my
brothers, had been good, even honourable, that they had given over
the largest parts of their own lives to us. I suddenly understood the
pain I must have caused them in my struggle to form myself.

I sat in the back, learning to smile, my small cup of life full of
happiness and love.

*

At Lorne the good weather held and the sea glittered. My body felt as if it had recently been unwrapped from too-heavy clothing, I felt like a newly shorn lamb. I stood on the hotel balcony looking out at the sea and the sky; the air smelt fresh and delicious. 'I'm going for a swim,' I announced. 'It's not Queensland, you know,' said my mother.

Striding along the path by the sea I felt lucky. I had my baby, a man I loved, my writing, a whole world. From this distance it struck me that all the difficulties Les and I had been through were little ones, and to fix them would only be a simple matter of re-arranging our ways of looking. It seemed to me that it didn't matter if my writing never provided me with a flourishing income, that it must be possible to find a way out of our money troubles. We already had everything we could wish for and it was only the way we looked at things that would have to change.

Striding along the path my body felt returned to me. I knew I still had a fistula, but it was something I had learnt to live with. Since I had begun a rigorous pelvic floor exercise program and no longer suffered constipation, any problems with rectal wind were minor.

As I plunged into the cold sea, joy slapped in my blood.

I see now I was at that dangerous point where I believed I would never be unhappy again.

Les and I had discussed whether Caspar was to be an only child. We both thought that one child was all we could handle, that we could provide Caspar with everything he needed both emotionally and materially. The thought of having two children struck me at least as overwhelming. I thought if I had another child I would never write anything again.

And yet ... and yet I didn't feel completely comfortable with the idea of having an only child either. I knew there were more of them about these days, but in my heart I had a creeping suspicion that it probably suited the parents more than the child. In one of Caspar's favourite books there were drawings of brothers and sisters. I always felt a twinge of sadness for him when he stared at them.

After Lorne we travelled to Ballarat and stayed in the hotel where Nellie Melba sang. I opened the door to its empty ballroom and walked around the silent room, admiring the wood panelling of the walls, the chandeliers. I thought of the goldfields, my great-great-grandmother who was supposed to be a French singer and who lost three children, drowned in a dam on the goldfields. She had lived in a tent.

I thought of the statue to my great-great-grandfather in Beechworth, the mad miner who had sent out buckets of champagne to his men in the fields after a lucky strike and who had his favourite horse shod in shoes of gold.

I was thinking of a novel, I was thinking of the past and how I might birth a new story.

Sometime over those few days, Caspar started to refuse every breastfeed. He cried and turned his head away as if I were offering him poison, he spat out the nipple as if it were his least favourite food.

I couldn't believe that after all we had been through, after finally getting him to sleep through the night, getting him to put on weight by having a supplementary feed of formula from his training cup, having him feed at my breast in relative calm at last, that after all this he was going to re-write the rules again.

I told you he was my ultimate Zen test.

My strategy consisted of starving him out, taking away all supplementary fluids until he gave in.

Back in Melbourne, my parents gone, Les quietly brought my opponent in to me as I lay waiting, turned on my side on the bed.

After the fifth day of refusing to feed, Caspar spontaneously opened his mouth and started to suck.

Back in Melbourne, together again, the three of us dwelt like fruits on the same stem. We slept, ate together, bathed together, began to slowly form ourselves into a new shoot of the family tree. That is, after eight months of daily life together, we were finally getting used to each other.

Then, just days after Caspar started to crawl, I peed into a glass jar and placed a pregnancy testing wand in it.

I was pregnant again, just when I had begun to see light.

The first thing I thought of after the shock was what was going to happen to the fistula.

8

A Good Pair of Hands

A body cupping a body
does not make two
that would be an error
too grave to be borne
given your season.

MEENA ALEXANDER,
YOUNG SNAIL

From the first this new pregnancy went badly. I felt sick all the time, sicker than I ever had with Caspar, and tired to the bone. I could hardly move from the bed or the chair where I sat down and only the need of a toilet bowl in which to vomit propelled me into action.

Caspar's needs compelled me to keep standing upright when I preferred to lie prone, to keep preparing his dinners when the smell of food nauseated me, to wash his clothes and hang them out to dry lest the washing assume the shape of a mountain impossible to conquer.

Although I was depressed at the thought of another baby, my mind reared back from the idea of abortion: I was still too close to Caspar's ruddy birth, the smell of vernix and amniotic fluid and blood was still fresh in my nostrils. My skin remembered the first sweet slap of new flesh against it.

I wondered how this baby had come to us. Oh, I knew all right the practical details of egg meeting sperm, but I wondered why it had taken months of careful planning to fall pregnant with Caspar while this new baby had conceived himself almost despite us. I hadn't even had a proper period.

It tempts every parent to look back on a pregnancy and imbue the born child's personality upon it. Elliot is like a force of nature, unpreventable, like weather.

For weeks I felt as if a great weight was pressing down on me. I couldn't conjure up any enthusiasm for the coming baby. All I could think of was my head going under again, of that long, deep dive I would have to take beneath the water. It was as if I knew I would have to walk out into the ocean with no alternative but to drown.

I couldn't even manage to summon up the anxiety about Down's

Syndrome which had so obsessed me during Caspar's pregnancy, and which I knew must be an even greater risk now because I was a year and a bit older. I was too depressed to bother worrying.

It seemed to me that I had only recently grown used to managing one child, and would find myself completely incapable of managing two.

Two children was beginning to look suspiciously like a proper family. I didn't know whether I could see myself in this picture.

At eleven weeks I had an ultrasound. There he was (for I could not help feeling it was a boy even though I surprised myself by finding a small, growing hope that I would have a girl).

He was alive all right, a pulsing, flailing creature represented on a screen above my head. 'Look, Cappy, there's a bubba,' I said to Caspar who was also in the room.

'Bubba,' he answered, barely glancing at the screen.

'Bubba,' I said and somewhere inside myself I opened a door.

This time around I did not go around madly buying up every baby thing I could find. At some point we borrowed a bassinet (we had sold the Emmaljunga ensemble), I dug out all Caspar's baby clothes from the plastic bag in the wardrobe and cleared a space in my head for a picture of myself with two babies, sixteen months apart.

As soon as I could I made an appointment to see the obstetrician I had already consulted about the fistula. We still had no private medical insurance but I wondered how much it was going to cost if she delivered me privately.

'Well, dear, firstly I don't take on uninsured patients. I can give you the names of a couple of people who do, though,' she said. I knew she was also a consultant at one of Melbourne's better public maternity hospitals and I asked for her opinion on registering there as a public patient.

'Certainly you would be in good hands,' she said, 'but I think the more important question is how you should be delivered. My advice is that you've already suffered enough trauma to the vaginal area and you should have a caesarean section.'

'But you won't do it personally?'

'My secretary will give you the names and addresses of some very good obstetricians who will.'

The consultation was clearly over. 'Don't worry, dear, you can have the fistula repaired at a later date,' she said at the door.

I left, beginning my search for a good pair of hands.

What if I had handsomely paid a doctor to deliver me by caesarean section? What if I had insisted on nothing but the knife on my stomach? Would the earlier knife have prevented the later knife from slicing open my gut and pulling up a bright, slippery loop of bowel to the surface?

What if? What if? What if?

I registered as a public patient, basing my decision on the fact that the hospital had the very same doctors working as consultants whom I would be paying as a private patient. I had access to them all, in one of the city's best teaching hospitals and, besides, we didn't have a lot of money to spare.

The first doctor I saw did the usual weighing checks, urine checks for pregnancy diabetes and so forth and asked me details about the last delivery and the fistula. After he examined me, asking if I'd ever suffered faecal soiling and other questions, I dressed and sat down opposite him.

'I can't see any reason why you shouldn't deliver vaginally,' he said. 'You're healthy, you don't have any other obstetric complications, and your last labour and birth was perfectly straightforward, apart from the third-degree tear and subsequent fistula. I'd advise a vaginal delivery.'

I looked at him. 'But the specialist I saw advised a caesarean. She said there was already too much trauma to the area.'

The doctor smelt strongly of tobacco. 'Well, yes, that's one opinion. I just think that a caesarean is unnecessary, it's an added complication, plus the recovery period is not inconsequential. There's really no obstetric reason for one.'

I was tired, confused. 'Thank you,' I said, 'I'll have to think about it.'

Outside in the lobby, full of women huge with child, weighing themselves, reading magazines, clearly divided between those first-timers with dreams in their eyes and mothers delivered to wild reality, outside in that lobby I tried to gather my thoughts.

After a while I joined the appointments queue. Fifteen, twenty minutes later, I finally reached the woman at the desk. I handed her my appointment card. 'I'd like to request another doctor please. I want a second opinion. Can I see the head of the clinic at my next appointment?'

She looked at the computer screen. '9.30 or 9.45? That's all I've got left for the Wednesday clinic.'

'9.45 will be fine,' I said. Then I went to pick up Caspar from the hospital creche.

My belly grew quickly. I had not lost all the excess weight from my first pregnancy, and by my fourth month I already looked ready to deliver. The bones of my face lurked somewhere in the flesh, a memory only. I felt unhealthy, puffed by the smallest set of stairs, unbelievably tired. 'Perhaps I'm giving birth to a changeling,' I said to Les. 'Hhmm, a small wrestler,' he replied.

Les felt weighed down too, by the idea of another child, by the feeling of lack of movement in his life. We began to talk seriously again about buying a house, but both of us felt felled by the idea of permanent exile in suburbia.

We tried to talk about what our fears were exactly when we pictured ourselves in a house with a lawn and a fence. I admit that when I was younger I had a kind of mild contempt for those lives lived behind the safe bars of good citizenship, but now I saw in those same lives a kind of integrity.

In all truth, I didn't know anymore what made me think I was any different to a person who wished to live peacefully in a house with a lawn and a fence. I mean, I was hardly a revolutionary myself, with a bomb in my hand and a plan to cause anarchy. I was hardly a bohemian, into Ecstasy and sleeping rough. I was a middle-class woman, a feminist who had chosen to marry and have children.

It was just that I could not bear to give up the notion that my whole life had now been decided, as if a great final line had been drawn under everything.

As winter approached, we started to look seriously at property. We didn't look at houses, though, we looked at warehouses, units with rooftop gardens, anything which did not have a fence with a gate to suggest we had fenced ourselves in.

One Saturday, Les rang me from a phone booth. I could tell at once he was excited. 'Where is it?' I asked and we made arrangements to meet.

The warehouse had once been a theatre, but no-one knew if there was a ghost. It had soaring ceilings, two bathrooms and, best of all, an outside terrace for children. In Sydney it would cost half a million but in Melbourne it cost less than half that, and in the car on the way back we did our sums. It was more than we wanted to pay, but Les was in love.

Only weeks after we moved in, we went up to Queensland on an extended trip combining both work and a holiday we had pre-arranged months before. *Hungry Ghosts* was being published, and I was expected to do media interviews and to take part in the Brisbane Writers' Festival, to begin the task of 'impersonating myself', to use Robert Dessaix's witty phrase.

The speed with which books are turned over in bookshops these days means you have a very small window of time in which to sell your book. There is a short blast of trumpets, as much fanfare as the publishers can whip up, and then there is silence.

Caspar and I flew up to Queensland ahead of Les, joining my parents at a holiday house on Bribie Island.

Caspar had been standing on his own for a few weeks now, an expression of pleasure on his little Les face. He was generally pleased with himself all round, happy to hold onto fingers and be assisted around the garden. He loved the water too, and playing in the sand, hearing the kookaburras. He especially loved each set of grandparents and all his cousins, and when I watched them playing together I knew we had made the right decision in coming back to Australia.

After a few days my father had to go into hospital for a minor operation and Caspar and I were left alone to await Les's arrival.

I was very excited on the afternoon he arrived and ran straight out to the hire car when I saw him pull up. Caspar was in my arms, but he seemed to have forgotten his father already.

'It's Dadda,' I said, bending forward so Les could give him a kiss. I felt a gush of blood between my legs as I moved and my eyes must have registered something.

'What's wrong?' said Les.

'I'm bleeding,' I said.

Within ten minutes we were all in the hire car on the way to the local hospital on the mainland. I cried all the way, certain that I had lost the baby. I was huge, I was twenty-one weeks, well out of the first trimester when most miscarriages occur. I wondered if I would have to deliver a dead baby.

In the emergency room I was examined, given an ultrasound, a pad on which to bleed, and told that the placenta appeared to be attached to the front of the uterine wall and that if I kept the baby for the next couple of hours, everything would probably be all right. Chances were high though that I would go into premature labour. The baby was not mature enough to survive.

I lay awake all night, suddenly desperate to see my baby's face.

The next morning the doctor came to examine me. 'How's the bleeding?' As I sat up in bed, the baby gave a hearty kick.

'I'm still spotting,' I said, 'but the baby's moving.'

'Good-oh,' he said, 'let's have a look.'

He placed one of those hearing things to my stomach and the baby's heartbeat could be heard, loud, regular, strong.

'Sounds pretty good to me,' he said. 'In most cases the baby pushes the placenta up into the right position as it grows. If you don't get any more bleeding I wouldn't be too worried. See your doctor when you get back to Melbourne.'

'Is it safe to fly?' I was supposed to fly down and back to Sydney in one day the following week: a television book show wanted to do an interview.

'You'll have to decide that yourself,' he said.

I didn't fly to Sydney for the interview. A live baby suddenly seemed more important to me than selling an extra copy of an inanimate book.

I had missed the short blasts of trumpets.

Several days later, in Brisbane, I began to impersonate myself. I impersonated myself as the editor of *WomenLoveSex* (which had also recently been published) at a writer's panel on the theme of women, love and sex with the poet Dorothy Porter and novelists Thea Astley and Linda Jaivin.

Thea was her usual brilliant self, dryly commenting on the duty of modern novelists to write about sex and how dull she found it, Linda delivered a wonderful speech about her fantasies of corgis and cream and transgressing boundaries, Dorothy read out an explicit poem about anal sex by Allen Ginsberg, warning the audience before she started that if they found explicit sexual writing offensive they should leave at once.

I lumbered over to the microphone and attempted a joke about myself being a woman with obvious intimate knowledge of the workings of heterosexual sex. 'I might only have carnal knowledge of a turkey baster though,' I said and only a few people smiled. I suddenly noticed a lot of dykes in the audience.

Before I knew it Thea and myself had been painted into the conservative redneck corner and Linda and Dorothy were fighting for everyone who lived on the margins, free of marriage, children and suburbia.

Clearly, the majority had conscripted me while I wasn't paying attention.

One afternoon during that extended stay in the sun Caspar had his last breastfeed. Ever since I'd fallen pregnant my milk supply had tapered off even further and by now he was only having one feed a day.

I remember exactly what that last feed was like. He was all wriggly and I had trouble getting him to settle. I was feeding him on a bed under a window, turned on my side. He looked up at me, smiling, and then he gave me a great, whopping bite.

'Ouch!' I said, pulling away. He was laughing like anything. 'OK, you win,' I said. I grabbed him, giving him a tickle, and any grief about the loss of one particular closeness was submerged in laughter.

While we were still in Brisbane Caspar had his first birthday. Les had already gone back to Melbourne, to the depths of winter, but Caspar and I stayed on in the warmth.

A few days before his birthday he walked up the hallway by himself. He was resting against the wall most of the way, but nevertheless he was propelling himself on his own two legs. His legs were placed very wide apart so that he looked as if he was straddling air.

He could take a few steps without the aid of a wall too, and before Les went back he had enjoyed walking unsteadily between my arms and Les's as we crouched close together on the floor. He repeated his steps again and again: the rush towards Les, the rush back towards me, the triumph each time he landed.

He was learning the art of balancing within the fences of our arms.

He was one year old, born to the air for three hundred and sixty five days. He was himself alone, standing on his own two legs, the recipient of my donated sleep, my anger, frustration and love.

He was my benefactor of happiness.

9

Last Days on Dry Land

The children are growing out
of me, wider than trees or rooms —

JUDITH RODRIGUEZ,
THE RUGS

Back in Melbourne trees were in bud. The sun was higher in the sky and its rays finally penetrated the windows of our warehouse. Already we knew we had made another mistake in buying it (we had attempted to rectify our first mistake by trading in the second-hand blue bomb for a reliable new car, but had to take out a hefty personal loan to do it).

Now, at night in our bedroom on the mezzanine floor of our new warehouse, we found we could hear the snores of our neighbours above us, hear the creak of their futon as they rolled over in bed. We felt we had no privacy lying in our own bed, as if there was only the flimsiest of screens separating us. When our female neighbour wore high heels on the polished floors we could track her every step and we could sometimes hear snippets of conversations.

Luckily our neighbours proved to be the considerate kind and we soon became friends; they knew about the noise problems already (the previous owners frequently played loud music and they often overheard entire conversations). Consequently our neighbours rarely wore shoes when they were home, but on those (thankfully) rare occasions when they had guests it was like a herd of elephants in Cuban heels.

We discovered too that the entire complex was riddled with sound problems, that air vents had been blocked off where they shouldn't (so that I could always smell what our friends upstairs were having for dinner) and that the Body Corporate was rent by faction fighting. Several residents in the block were no longer speaking to each other.

Basically, it was a case of greedy developers doing a sloppy job, getting in before governments and councils caught up with warehouse developments and began issuing edicts. There were compensations though: we quickly made friends both inside the complex and in the surrounding area, and Caspar adored the two bigger boys across the courtyard.

In my seventh month of pregnancy the muscles in my back parted like a curtain. One morning I could not get out of bed and when Les finally helped me up, every step I took was difficult: it took me a full ten minutes to get down the stairs. Coincidentally my appointment at the hospital was due that day, and I tottered in to see the head of the clinic like some arthritic eighty-five-year-old woman.

'What's happened to you?' he said as I made my way awkwardly through the doorway.

'I'm falling apart,' I replied. The thought suddenly struck me that as I was in a lot of pain I could be in early labour. The doctor assisted me up onto the examination table and examined me.

'This happens sometimes with two pregnancies so close together. Your poor old back probably hasn't recovered from the first pregnancy. Did you have problems last time?'

'I've never had a back problem in my life,' I said.

Several hours later I emerged from the hospital with a kind of weightlifter's belt velcroed low on my stomach beneath the great mass of baby. The hospital physiotherapist had measured me, too, for a kind of pregnancy corset, a stretchy elastic garment intended to hold everything together. And the doctor had ordered some blood tests because I was so enormous, and he wanted to discount the possibility of late onset pregnancy diabetes (which can cause abnormally large babies).

Placental bleeding, parted back muscles, fistulas, big babies, personal loan debts, no privacy in our own bed: the circumstances of my life were not exactly conducive to confidence. Oh, and I forgot to tell you that my English publisher didn't want to publish *Hungry Ghosts* on the grounds that it was 'too accessible' and not really 'our kind of book'. Besides wounding my confidence, the reality of this meant my annual income was depleted by some fifteen thousand dollars. If I was the superstitious type I would have said the omens for the impending birth were not auspicious.

The head of the clinic agreed with the other doctor on his staff. 'I can see your specialist's point about a caesarean,' he said, 'but in my opinion that's being overly cautious. I always like to see vaginal deliveries wherever possible and I think in your case if there's an elective episiotomy there shouldn't be any problems.'

'So if you control the possibility of another third-degree tear everything should be OK?'

I thought the doctor had exceptionally long fingernails for a man, and especially for a man whose gloved fingers were inserted in a woman's most tender parts during the day. I wondered if he had even noticed.

'Look,' he said, putting a special red sticker on my medical history, 'I'll write it all up in the notes that you're to have an elective episiotomy. They'll know all about you the moment you walk in the door.'

I looked at him uncertainly. 'And you have full confidence that a vaginal delivery is the best way to go?'

He smiled. 'Yes.'

He was a highly regarded obstetrician. He was the second doctor who thought I should be delivered vaginally. I did not want to undergo a caesarean if it was truly unnecessary, for part of me was terrified at the thought of one. I was trying to make an informed decision, but I had to admit I was also a layperson who did not have a medical degree.

'I guess I'll just have to have confidence in your confidence then,' I said.

I wondered why I didn't feel any.

Caspar began to speak his first words, other than Mama, Dada and Bubba. 'Bus,' he said, having some trouble with the 's'. 'Car' he said and we clapped, causing him to say it again. 'Stop,' he said, forgetting the 's' completely; and then he began inventing his own words.

'Gobima' was his favourite, all purposeful, muttered under his breath and at speaking volume, indicating toys, food, pleasure. We laughed when he said it and incorporated it into our own speech, going to the 'yops' to buy bread, milk and gobima.

But most significant of all was when he learnt to say 'more'. He said it when he wanted more food, more time in the bath, another several hours on the swings.

It was his password to life, an acknowledgement of the possibilities of existence.

He was wanting more you see, more of everything: he was saying yes to life.

Because of my back problems I could not pick Caspar up, do any lifting or even hang out the washing. There was no alternative but to get someone in to help again, and luckily Carol was temporarily available. It was wonderful to have her, but my money was running out and Les and I started to argue about money again. I felt ashamed of the arguing, embarrassed to think we were being overheard by our neighbours. I thought I should have more self-control, more dignity.

I couldn't afford to pay Carol at $10 an hour for much longer. I had recently heard about family day care, significantly cheaper than home help and provided I could find the right carer it sounded like a reasonable alternative. The scheme, run by local councils, provides carefully selected care-givers who mind a small number of babies and children in their own homes.

I expected to go through several candidates before I found the right carer, but to my surprise we chose the first and only one we met. Consuelo and her family were from El Salvador, and their youngest child was only a few weeks older than Caspar. The two babies looked each other over and immediately turned away to inspect more interesting toys on the floor. Consuelo laughed, a hearty, engaging laugh, and I immediately felt she was the right one.

After a trial afternoon where Caspar waved me off happily and did not want to go home when I arrived to pick him up, I decided to try him at Consuelo's two days a week.

At fourteen months, Caspar officially began family day care: he had a little bag which carried his milk, his lunch, his nappies, a change of clothes. Consuelo had the number of our doctor in case of emergency and was, in effect, responsible for Caspar's care, safety and comfort for all the hours he was not in front of my eyes.

When I dropped him off for the first time he clung to me, crying, and I had to peel him off before I could close the door behind me. As I slowly and painfully manoeuvred myself into the car, tears welled in my eyes and I thought of my mother's disapproval of women who had children at the last minute as a kind of modern life accessory, only to dump them later on someone else to look after.

I kept picturing Caspar's stricken face before me on the drive home, and almost turned the car around. Only the thought of my painful back and all the remaining baby chores I still had to do prevented me from doing it. As soon as I got home I rang Consuelo.

'Oh, he's OK,' she said cheerily. 'He did not cry anymore after you go. He's playing now.' I could hear him making noises in the background, busy again with his own life.

As I put the phone down I felt racked with guilt. At the same time I also heard the quiet of the space around me, and felt a small, guilty pleasure at the thought of opening a cupboard without a fight, at being able to sit down and drink a cup of tea while it was still hot.

Daringly, I thought I might even read the newspaper.

As day by day Caspar grew, he began to test the boundaries of himself. He wanted to know how far he extended into the world, what his own will could and could not do, for he had begun to sense his own powers. While he did not as yet comprehend the fact that if he scaled his bookcase like a rock climber it would fall on top of him, he had certainly begun to perceive, for example, that he could resist being strapped into his highchair. He sensed that if he screamed and thrashed about wildly enough it wrought some change in me, sometimes even causing me to wrest him angrily from the highchair and dump him hard on the floor, still kicking and screaming. It was clear that he did not know exactly what his resistance was for, except that it somehow distinguished himself from me and my intentions.

Caspar began to refuse to get dressed, to get undressed, to get into the car, into the stroller, to get into the bath and out again. We referred to him in mock Russian as the refusnik, and tried to laugh about it. More usually though it took all my self-control and imagination to distract him, to ease him gently into whatever action I had planned for him. More usually I got angry myself until I learnt to take a deep breath and remind myself that I was the adult testing ground and he was the child rocket practising blast-off.

When he got into whinge mode, though, I was tested to the limit.

He was a champion whinger, able to whinge non-stop for hours, ceaseless as monsoonal rain. At such moments I wanted to shake him until his teeth rattled, to shut him up, to stop him from ruining my life. At such moments I could not remember the joy he had brought me and motherhood seemed only a burden.

As the birth grew closer I was sometimes struck by a piercing sadness when I looked at Caspar, when the three of us were sitting quietly together in the moments before he went to bed. Sometimes my eyes filled with tears when I thought about us living our last days together as just us three, the last moments of Caspar being the pivot of our lives.

I felt sorry for him. A first child myself, he struck me as only a baby, too young to be tipped from the basket, and it seemed to me that his time in the light had been too brief. I was flooded by memories of my own jealousies of my brothers, the fights we had right up till late adolescence, and how only now, at almost forty, did I know I loved them without reservation.

This feeling of love for my own brothers eased my fears over Caspar's approaching loss. For although he was undoubtedly going to be saddened by the diversion of my full attention, I knew that love was multifarious, its fire never ending, and this new baby would bring fresh kindling for its flames.

As the year came to a close, a race of sorts began between the baby and my fortieth birthday. I was due to turn forty on December 30, the second last day of the year (a birthday which everyone has trouble remembering, coming as it does hot on the heels of

Christmas and the day before New Year's Eve). I was too tired and it was too hot to plan a party, and none of my closest friends were in Melbourne anyway. I wondered if the baby would arrive while I was still thirty-nine, or perhaps even turn up as a birthday present.

Then, just before Christmas, a woman I had previously known in a professional capacity as a book editor invited me to her book group's Christmas dinner. I didn't know anyone, but Maryann made me feel welcome, and by the time I drove home at the end of the night I was exhilarated as though I had drunk too much champagne. Here was a group of women with whom I knew straight away I could be friends: mothers, workers, artists, singers, musicians, all passionate about books and ideas. I couldn't stop talking, and felt dangerously manic, as if I had recently returned from the desert to people who spoke my own tongue. I suddenly sensed the possibility of belonging.

In the few weeks left to me before the baby's birth I was surprised by a sudden burst of energy. I madly went around washing and folding the last of the baby clothes, preparing the bassinet, finally getting the futon repaired and re-covered. I got a couple of quotes from cabinet makers about building a bookcase into the wall to house all my books, I finally had some filing cabinets and shelves built into the mezzanine office space outside our bedroom. I was in that fevered last dash before being swept out to sea, I could already smell the salt in my nostrils.

The baby inside me swelled and rolled, my breasts began to leak fluid. I was heading for the water; I sensed the water rising in me.

This time I fully understood that I was living my last days on dry land.

10

Life's Darling

As the old hermit of Prague, that never saw pen
and ink, very wittily said to a niece
of King Gorboduc,
'That that is is.'

SHAKESPEARE,
TWELFTH NIGHT

As the sun was going down on the evening of January 8, 1997, I felt a few painless contractions. By now, everyone I knew made jokes about me giving birth to a baby elephant, about thirteen-month-long pregnancies, about babies going on strike and refusing to be born. The baby was late, I was forty years and nine days old exactly, and I felt as if I had been pregnant forever.

The contractions were nothing like I had experienced with Caspar, and I was not even sure I was in labour. I felt gripped, the muscles of my abdomen pulled tight yet it was curiously painless, like a warm-up exercise. Only the date on the calendar made me ring the hospital; the midwife suggested a cup of tea.

We had arranged with Katrina, a new friend from across the courtyard, to stay with Caspar if needed until Tracey came. Tracey was the only friend I knew in Melbourne when we first arrived, the mother of two young sons who was now recovering from post-natal depression. Our mothers were best friends and Tracey was the closest thing to family. Katrina wasn't home, but when I rang Tracey she said she'd come as soon as she could. I left a message on Katrina's answer phone.

Les came home and made us both a cup of herbal tea while Caspar played with blocks on the floor. I felt calm, slightly foolish for having rung Tracey when I wasn't even sure what was happening. As I sat on the couch drinking tea in my thin summer dress the tightenings went on: when my belly was gripped by one I could see the shape of the baby through the material. I felt no pain.

'I think I'll have a bath,' I said. Caspar got up to follow me but Les restrained him. 'Mama! Mama!' he screamed, but I was already on my way to the bathroom. I felt strangely detached from everything.

In the bath the tightenings continued and I watched with amazement. Whenever they came I saw the whole body of the baby, the curve of the spine, the shape of a rump. My skin was a palimpsest on which a new language was being written; beneath its surface a fresh heart was already learning to transcribe.

Only centimetres away from my forty-year-old skin, with its history of love and betrayal and tenderness, with my entire lived life written upon it, a virgin life was in motion, blood flowing, eyes seeing, ears already listening for sound. An unblemished skin was itself waiting to be written upon, so close and yet hidden within me. With my hands I cupped my baby, that is to say I cupped myself: I was at once both vessel and cargo, one yet also two.

Giving birth changed me forever. Those two bodies who lived within me now live without, but they will always be part of me as long as I am alive and sentient, like some lost part of my own self. My body will always remember the imprint of theirs, the way all my organs were pressed flat, causing my heart to turn.

I have been fully occupied, my sons' claimed land. I was once a single, monolithic entity, but now I am broken open, all my walls have been breached. My womb might be empty but I swear to you my body and heart remember every single thing.

Katrina arrived at the same time as Tracey. 'What's happening?' they both asked together. 'Oh, goody,' said Tracey, 'I've always wanted to call out, "Bring me some boiling water!"'

I laughed and the three of us went inside to find Les had already put the kettle on for more tea. We sat around while my stomach continued to alternately grow tight and relax painlessly. 'I'm still not sure …' I said, and Tracey came over to have a feel.

'Feels like a contraction to me,' she said. 'Why don't you go up to the hospital anyway?' Just then I noticed a slightly stronger contraction.

'It's still not hurting,' I said doubtfully. I went upstairs to get my bag anyway, excitement suddenly breaking open inside me as I mounted the stairs.

At the hospital as we were getting out of the car I felt the first painful contraction. I doubled over on the pavement.

'This is it,' I said, beginning to walk fast across the road, trying to get inside the hospital doors before the next contraction came.

'My name's Susan Johnson,' I said to the admissions nurse calmly. 'I'm having my second baby. Here's my card.'

I should have screamed, 'MY NAME'S SUSAN JOHNSON AND I'VE GOT A RECTO-VAGINAL FISTULA. I NEED A CAESAREAN NOW!'

I didn't, of course. I thought they would know all about me from my medical records, those medical records with the large reassuring red dot. I am the type of person whose first instinct is to trust authority: I am not a cynic by nature and I have had to learn cynicism through my own mistakes. I do not instinctively distrust the police.

My mother thinks I am naive and I have always felt offended by this, implying as it does a native stupidity. Privately I have always felt myself to be a shrewd and cunning kind of person, occasionally underestimated. I know all my faults too well: overweening pride, a tendency towards paranoia, secretive, competitive, inclined to envy, occasionally self-important, with a sad ability to boast.

Of my attributes I am less sure. Certainly I like to think of myself as sensitive to others, even perceptive, and have on occasion prided myself on having a fine nose for liars and bullshit artists, for poseurs and charlatans. In other words I believed myself to be the opposite of naive, and sometimes even considered myself to have a certain savvy.

Yet now, whenever I picture myself standing at that labour ward admissions desk, I see only my stupid, naive face. I see myself offering my body up trustingly, in good faith, a foolish girl willing to believe.

I stood at that admissions desk like an obedient child. If part of becoming an adult means an ability to test every truth for oneself, I was belatedly standing on the threshold of adulthood, a forty-year-old woman having her second baby.

These days I test every supposed truth I come across. If I was ever naive I have lost it for good, and have not even cared to seek out my mother's opinion.

And this is what I ask myself now: is naivety a form of arrogance, its dark, flip side, a stupid, childlike belief that life will treat you kindly as a matter of course? Isn't it a form of arrogance to assume that misfortune will not personally visit you, or to allow yourself to believe the man who says his love for you is endless as space?

Why did I think I would always be life's darling, eternally safe from harm? Where did I get the idea that it would always be you sitting in the wheelchair or slumped in front of the telly in the nursing home and only myself still standing? Why did I think it would always be you with the colostomy bag?

Now I know that only a breath separates me from you, myself from the wheelchair, from disabling disease, from stroke, from death itself. If once I asked Why me?, now I would never be so presumptuous, so gloriously, naively arrogant. Why not me? Each and every one of us is making private moves in the same direction, the only difference being that some moves are more public than the rest.

Up on the labour ward I was placed in a small anteroom to await developments. Slightly larger than a cupboard, the room was hot and airless, and straight away I became obsessed with getting onto the TENS equipment (a popular form of pain relief in Sweden, transcutaneous electrical nerve stimulation works by interrupting pain transmission via a small electric current transmitted through a series of electrodes stuck on your lower back). I knew it was vital to get hooked up in early labour before contractions become too intense.

'We'll see about your TENS after the midwife has seen you,' said the nurse. As soon as she left the room I looked at Les and sighed.

He smiled. 'She looks like that German woman out of *The Baghdad Cafe*,' he said. 'I keep expecting her to burst into song.'

The woman might have been listening at the door because she immediately came back into the room. 'Now, where did I leave my stethoscope?' she said, her large bosom remaining obediently immobile as she lifted various objects around the room.

'Ouch,' I said, 'have you checked with the midwife yet?' The pains were coming hard and fast. I was already finding sitting up on the bed uncomfortable. 'I need to get onto that equipment as soon as I can.'

'Yes, dear,' she said absent-mindedly.

I got up off the bed and began to walk around the room. The walls were plastered with posters, and already I had forgotten that I should be telling everyone about the fistula, about the elective episiotomy: all I could think about was getting hooked up to the TENS equipment we had hired in advance and away from the pain that had invaded me.

'Where is it, Les? Can you go and see if it's coming?' I begged, between pains. 'They don't have a bath here, do they? I wish I could lie down in water.' Walking back and forth between the closed window and the door my eye took in a poster about cot death and the mysterious number 30,000 scrawled in pen on the wall. '30,000 what?' I asked no-one in particular. 'Where is that bloody machine?'

'When the midwife comes and says it's OK, dear. You don't want to get on too early,' said the German to me.

'But the whole *point* is to get on early,' I replied, trying not to scream. I didn't know how long I'd been in that hot room.

Suddenly the midwife was there and I was back on the bed, and the electrodes were stuck onto my lower back and the control device was in my hand. I turned it up full blast. I felt pins and needles in my lower back and wanted to blast my body to smithereens. 'It's not working,' I said, beginning to cry, and the contractions went from fifteen minutes apart to four minutes then two, and were quickly becoming unbearable. 'We'd better get to the delivery room,' the midwife said, and I looked into her eyes long enough to register that I liked her face.

On the walk to the delivery room I heard the sound of water and someone asked if I'd like a shower. The electrodes were peeled off, and I was standing under the water but the pain was coming at me too hard, causing my knees to buckle.

'OK, OK,' said the kind face, helping me out.

In the new room I found myself in the corner being held up under the arms by Les, and I noticed it was night and a blue light was flashing somewhere below on a cobbled street. 'What's that light?' I asked and suddenly a giant fist punched straight up my vagina, impaling me, skewering me to my own pain. I thought: I have gone mad, and heard my own voice begin to wail, my own voice crying out for an epidural, for more gas, for God. And I heard Les saying, 'Susan, look at me. Susan, BREATHE.' And miraculously I did, I looked at him and breathed and I was helped to the bed and a young doctor asked if I was to have an elective episiotomy and I said yes and I lay beached on the bed waiting for the slice of the knife, holding onto the midwife's hand, looking into her eyes, prepared to follow her to my own death. She was guiding my child out of me and I could feel my body giving him up.

And then he was born and straight away I wanted to do it again. He was wet and dark and I knew him at once and held him to me and cried. I cried like the river I was, with all my banks broken and all my silt and sludge washed away. My eyes wept salty tears and my vagina wept salty blood, and I heard Les saying, *Susan, enough! Enough!* But I did not stop, I cried on and on, washing myself and our new son clean, weeping my own small river into the great sea of existence.

He was bigger than Caspar, 4.40 kilograms, but how curly was my new son's tongue, how warm his frog-legged huddle! He was all soft flesh and milk and he parted for me a second time that frail membrane between death and being. For a moment I knew again that this was the essence of being, this moment, this beating of blood, this tiny pulse, this glorious Now. It was five past one on the 9th of January.

Dwelling in all that glory, that fragrant place where I forgot my own name, I forgot to ask why they hadn't done the episiotomy. Unbelievably, all through the labour both Les and I had forgotten to remind them about the fistula and as my tears dried it became apparent that I had suffered another bad third-degree tear (torn again down to the anal sphincter muscle). A sudden flurry of discussions took place, the specialist on call that night was paged for his opinion, while I waited, bleeding, on the bed.

Finally another young doctor came to talk to me. 'The doctor thinks we should do a temporary repair now and leave the final repair of the fistula till later. There's a lot of bleeding and swelling around the area now.'

I asked her a few more questions, then Les and I looked at each other. 'What do you think?' I asked him. 'I'll leave you to have a talk,' the young doctor said, 'but we'd better get you stitched up at least temporarily.'

About fifteen minutes later my legs were up in stirrups, shaking uncontrollably, while the young doctor wielded her needle.

The damage was of course already done.

Now I will speak of this: in wrenching back childbirth from the hands of the (mostly) male doctors, in telling ourselves that our bodies instinctively know how to do it and that male doctors with their forceps and fondness for caesareans are the enemy of all birthing women, we forgot that birth involves danger, the loud, hot breath of the wolf.

Instead we blocked our ears and invented for ourselves a kind of earth-mother hierarchy, feeling ashamed, disappointed or even like failures if we resorted to pain relief or ended up with an emergency caesarean after being cheated of a vaginal delivery. We turned the experience of birth into our own private movie, casting ourselves in the starring role.

In truth we have turned our faces away from the fact that at each and every birth death hovers about the room, the silent presence. We do not wish to remember that babies die, strangled in their own cords only minutes from light, nor do we wish to dwell on the fact that women still bleed to death in distant rooms where there is no recourse to drugs designed to stop haemorrhaging.

In most first world countries, death is quickly ushered from the room. But even in your clean laundered bed you will still feel the rush of air against your skin as he passes. Even if your baby is delivered to you safe and whole, and your own body signs are still vital, you will not escape the faint brush of death's wing.

Forget him at your peril. Mother, salute him.

The morning after Elliot's birth another young doctor came to see me. By then I was already worried about the effect of another bad tear on the fistula, angry that I hadn't had the promised episiotomy and distressed about what was going to happen next.

The young doctor implied there had been mismanagement. 'They couldn't read the notes. Look, I'll arrange to get you on the operating list for the fistula repair.' She leaned closer. 'Confidentially, you can make a complaint. This sort of thing shouldn't happen. I know the doctor's angry that his instructions weren't carried out.'

Elliot whimpered and I picked him up. 'He promised me several times that everything would be written up in the notes.'

A nurse came into the room and the young doctor got up. 'As I said, I'll see if I can get you on the operating list.'

'Thanks,' I replied. As I laid Elliot down in his clear perspex cot, a rush of air escaped from my vagina.

*

Later that day a kindly midwife came to see me. 'I'm really sorry,' she said, 'it was a well-controlled delivery and there didn't seem the need for an episiotomy.'

She said that doctors' written notes often couldn't be deciphered.

'Why aren't they typed up instead?' I asked.

'It would cost too much, I suppose,' she said, leaning over to pat my hand. 'Don't worry too much, Susan. There's always a chance the fistula's been repaired. It happens, you know.'

I didn't tell her I already suspected it was worse.

On the third day after Elliot's birth, Les came to pick us up from the hospital.

Sometimes now I remember that drive home, the flailing newborn, the seventeen-month-old who did not appear to register his new brother's existence, Les driving calmly holding my hand, and myself, bleeding and worried. Yet curiously I was happy too, leaking tears and milk, and for one brief moment my life felt like a gift. It seemed in that moment that the weight in the car was perfectly balanced, as if some metaphysical law of measurement had been reached and we were magically a family.

I still like to think of this picture.

11

Elliot's Alphabet

Joy, but with fear yet link'd.

MILTON,
PARADISE LOST

If Caspar was a kind of language I had to learn, Elliot was an alphabet I recognised. From the first he seemed familiar to me, flesh of my flesh, a recognisable member of my tribe. I found I instinctively knew what he longed for most and whenever I picked him up he soon ceased crying.

It wasn't that he looked more like me than Les (although he did resemble my side of the family) but that I seemed able to intuitively meet his needs and therefore, reluctant as I am to admit it, he also met mine. I was so clearly his source of nourishment and comfort that I finally began to have some confidence in my abilities to mother. I felt rewarded.

Whether my ease in mothering him was the direct result of Elliot's own easy predictability or whether as a seasoned mother I was more relaxed I cannot say. In the cosmic baby lottery I had somehow been graced, and in those fearful months when my body failed me I sometimes wondered whether Elliot was not some heavenly compensation prize.

From the minute we got him home he slept for long uninterrupted blocks of time, giving me the chance to attend to other pressing things in my life besides him. He also fed effortlessly so that my breasts were always full of milk, and whenever he was awake he seldom cried.

I never rocked him to sleep once; instead he fell asleep anywhere and in any place, in slings, car seats, strollers, in his carry cot on the kitchen bench surrounded by Caspar's activities and noise. He quickly grew used to being dumped unceremoniously in Caspar's cot (the only room in the warehouse with a door) while I attended to Caspar or got dinner ready or folded the washing. He fed anywhere, too.

'Second child syndrome,' everyone said, nodding their heads as if there could be no doubt. Certainly I had less time to fret about him, and I witnessed first hand how leaving a baby to put himself to sleep is preferable to assisting him (poor Elliot never had a choice), yet I also know women who had far more difficult babies second time around.

It seems to me that a baby's temperament must also be considered. If I was more relaxed with Elliot it was partly because he demanded less of me, for he had a kind of sturdy, robust presence from the start.

It made me wonder how much Caspar suffered in his early days. Elliot's temperament might well be considered more easy-going than his brother's, but he has never experienced any of the needles, X-rays and early separations that Caspar endured.

Caspar is sensitive to the air, my darling boy, my first born son.

If I had been worried about how Caspar would react to being usurped I needn't have. For the first few weeks at least Caspar didn't take much notice at all of Elliot. Only when I was breastfeeding did he show any signs of jealousy, sometimes trying to pull Elliot's mouth away from the nipple. I quickly learnt to have a pile of books and toys next to me where Caspar could sit beside us and play.

The fact that Caspar had always been close to Les helped enormously. After we came home from hospital Les took a fortnight off, effectively taking up the slack, and together he and Caspar went out on long walks, to parks and cafes.

When Les returned to work my parents-in-law came to help, entertaining Caspar who loved them, and also running the house while I more or less permanently fed Elliot. They were too polite to say, but I'm sure they felt I was overdoing it (and indeed, unlike Caspar, Elliot was a vomiter and regularly spewed copious amounts of milk, partly because his stomach was too full).

But with this baby I felt confident: I didn't visit the baby nurse at all once the obligatory home visits were over, I didn't take my mother's advice about overfeeding (at another time she also came to stay and help out), in fact, I didn't listen to anyone.

Instead, I kept Elliot close and fed him when it suited, laid him in his bassinet at regular intervals, and had milky vomits down my shoulder for months. Once I was doing an interview with a journalist from *The Australian* and Elliot spewed what looked like two litres of milk clear across the room. Mercifully, he was what the baby nurses call 'a happy vomiter' and seemed to positively enjoy the experience.

Then, when Caspar had just turned eighteen months and everyone had gone home to Queensland, I awoke in the middle of the night to find Caspar standing by Elliot's cradle. 'Bubba,' he said, 'bubba 'leeping.'

'Yes, darling,' I replied, getting up to take him back to bed. He had never before scaled the sides of his cot, yet in one fell swoop he had not only climbed out of his cot and walked out of his room but climbed the stairs (which had no handrails) to the mezzanine floor and our bedroom.

After that he started appearing at Elliot's cradle at irregular intervals throughout the night. We couldn't work out how to prevent him from doing it.

Finally, in desperation, Les moved the futon from the loungeroom to Caspar's bedroom and slept there. Elliot moved from the cradle to Les's side of the bed where I could feed him at night without having to get up.

I am sure you understand the implications of this new configuration. Children have a way of sprouting up between you, seeds of love, suddenly grown. Never again would there be just the two of us in the same way as before.

We were all suddenly joined, a tracery of roots, irrevocably tangled in the soil.

Paradoxically, just at that moment when our children came between us, conquering us in our own bed, our bodies began to fight back, demanding compensation. While the babies slept in the bright light of day, our bodies privately engaged in that dance of the senses, collecting rewards. On those days when Les was not at work, or when he unexpectedly came home at lunchtime, our bodies remembered all over again how desire had guided us.

On those bright hot afternoons I felt unwrapped, newly discovered. Once, I wept in the crumpled, milk-stained bed, being still close to birth's numinous glow, knowing as I wept that I could actually feel the fistula for the first time.

I wondered whether the same act of love which had delivered our babies to us was now sabotaging my body amidst joy.

As I slowly emerged from the haze of the birth, I began to think more clearly about Elliot's delivery and what went wrong, and to consider the best repair. I see now that I was also resisting the idea that the fistula was worse and, indeed, when I made an early appointment to see the gynaecologist I had originally consulted regarding the fistula she was not even sure it was still present.

After she examined me she reported that I now had what she called a 'non-existent perineum'.

'What does that mean? That my vagina now meets my anus?'

She allowed herself a brief, grim smile. 'Not exactly,' she said, 'quite a few women are born with a very small area there anyway. I wouldn't worry about that at present, the main thing is to see whether or not you've still got a fistula.'

'I think I have,' I said.

'We'll see, dear, we'll see.' As she wrote up her notes I told her about the birth and the young doctor who had said she would put me on her operation waiting list if I still needed a repair.

'It's your decision, dear, but if you like I'll arrange for you to see the Professor. He's very experienced with recto-vaginal fistulas through his work in oncology.'

We discussed again the best time for a repair and she reiterated that she still felt the optimum time was when I had finished breast-feeding and my vagina was fully oestrogenised again.

'And even if you have still got a fistula you don't have to rush into a repair. You've lived with a fistula for what? A year? A year and a half? It won't hurt you to go on a bit longer.'

I suddenly felt panicked. 'But what about sex? I mean, it won't make the fistula larger or anything, will it?'

'It shouldn't, no,' she said. This reply did not sound definite enough to me.

I remember it was searingly hot that day, and when I went out into the waiting room, Les and Caspar were not there. After a long while I took the lift down to the ground floor and waited outside beneath a tree.

Elliot was asleep against my arm, his hair wet with sweat. I suddenly felt tired and alone.

Within weeks I knew for sure that the fistula was back. Air passed through my rectum and out my vagina regularly and I had great trouble controlling it. Also, whenever Les and I had sex I could keenly feel where the fistula must be. It didn't hurt exactly, but the whole area felt strange, as if there was only the flimsiest of tissue separating my vagina and anus. It seemed to me that the fistula must have got larger.

I rang the young doctor and left a message on her answer phone, thanking her and cancelling any plans she had made to include me on her operating list. I realised she was probably not much more than a registrar herself, and therefore relatively inexperienced. I did not want to risk anything else going wrong.

After a second appointment with the gynaecologist, who confirmed that the fistula was indeed present, her secretary gave me the Professor's details.

After ringing his office I was surprised that the Professor himself rang me back personally the same day. He had a pleasant voice and I took to it at once.

'Well then, you'd better come in and we'll have a look at you, Susan. What day suits you best?'

I like a professor who returns his own calls. Throughout our dealings he continued to ring me back as soon as he was able and once, in my darkest hour, I rang his home number on a Saturday night and left a long, rambling message on his answer machine.

By the time he returned my call on Sunday morning I had recovered some equilibrium. 'I'm sorry to have disturbed you at home on a Saturday night,' I said. 'It only occurred to me after I rang that you might have played my message back in the middle of a dinner party. Just what you need—an hysterical patient blathering on about her vagina coming apart!'

He laughed. 'Not at all, not at all, Susan,' he said kindly. 'You must ring any time you need to.'

That first morning, though, all I knew was that I liked the sound of the professor's voice and that he was going to give me back my old body.

*

As any woman who has given birth knows, however, I was never going to get back my old body, fistula or no fistula. I will bet you that in the privacy of their own bathroom mirrors even the stupendous Elle McPherson and that bosomy blonde woman from *Baywatch* could map the personal history of fruition and decay written upon their skin.

Babies leave visible traces, the silvery track of a stretchmark, the slack and shrivel of an emptied breast, the subtle darkening of a nipple. Your hair might mysteriously turn lighter or darker, or if it is curly it may inexplicably turn straight. The entire distribution of weight in your body may shift like one of those cloth dolls filled with sand.

A baby forces your body to open in a way it never has before, causing your very bones to move. I have heard of women who have popped blood vessels in their eyes while giving birth, of women developing varicose veins in their vaginas.

Even if you are safe from such extremes, your body will still tell your story. If it should ever be necessary that an autopsy be carried out on your body, your organs will reveal that they were once pressed flat and that your vagina once demonstrated its full capacity to deliver a life.

Have I also mentioned that because your body and your emotions are holding hands, every change to your body will resonate in your emotions? Your changed body will be electric with new or amplified feeling, as if your emotional repertoire has expanded.

I know women who say they didn't know what anger was until they had a baby, and dry-eyed women who now weep at the sight of starving children on the television news. I know women who have turned into terrible drivers when ferrying their babies because they suddenly have the emotional imagination to incorporate the vastness of loss.

I get all emotional now, a woman said to me the other night at Caspar's kindergarten orientation evening. She was worried she was going to cry at her daughter's first day at kindergarten.

I am warning you that after the birth of your baby, your laughter and rage and pain will be fuller, deeper, harder. You will suddenly see that the world is full of children, and there will be heartbreaking moments when you feel the full weight of each child's life as heavily as your own precious child's.

Several weeks after Elliot was born, I lay on the couch, spread my legs and used a large mirror to inspect the damage for myself.

Actually, things didn't look as bad as I had expected. I still had a good couple of inches between endings and beginnings, and I could not see anything remotely resembling a fistula. Only a very intimate friend would ever have known that things had once been any different.

After that I felt much better.

Les came with me to the first appointment to see the Professor. Elliot was with us too, in his blue travelling bassinet, and we balanced him carefully on some chairs in the corner. I could hear him making cooing noises through the curtain as the Professor examined me.

'I can see your fistula, Susan,' he said, poking around in the folds of my skin. 'It's rather low down.'

After I had dressed and attached Elliot to my breast the Professor explained that as fistulas went, mine was not in a particularly tricky area. In further conversation it became apparent that he had gleaned his expertise from women with mainly uterine or cervical cancers, where it was not uncommon for fistulas to form as tissue broke down. For the first time in some months I considered myself fortunate.

We discussed the pros and cons of waiting for the repair until I had finished breastfeeding. The Professor did not seem as convinced as my gynaecologist that hormone levels made much difference to healing. He agreed however that the constipation I seemed to suffer while breastfeeding (no matter how much water I drank or fruit and fibre I ate) should be considered.

The Professor then took a piece of paper from his desk and began to explain how the repair, called a Martius Graft, was carried out. He drew a neat little vagina and labial lips, explaining how a slice of the fatty outer labia would be sliced off and transferred to the area where the fistula was.

'That little pad of fat brings in new blood supplies to the area. If you can imagine, it's like a little cushion between the anus and vagina.'

'A bit like a skin graft?'

'Not quite, but close,' he said with a smile. 'Sometimes we do use a bit of skin if we need to, but not in your case. After you've had your surgery, we'll plug you up for a few days to ensure there's some healing to the wound before you pass any faeces. I'm sure you understand that one of the difficulties with this kind of surgery is that it's not a sterile area.'

'What do you intend to plug me up with?'

'Oh, a bit of codeine usually does the trick,' he said, smiling again. I liked him and found I instinctively trusted his judgement.

I wondered if he would give me the paper with the little drawing. As we left he said we should get in touch with him whenever we decided the time was right. As I didn't suffer faecal soiling, which left untreated can cause life threatening infections of the kidneys among other things, he didn't feel there was any particular urgency about a repair. I should ring him and give him a few weeks notice when I felt the time was right.

After hearing the actual details of the repair I suddenly didn't think there was any urgency either.

Unlike the early days with Caspar I was able to work while Elliot slept. On those days when Caspar was with Consuelo I sometimes even finished small pieces of writing.

In the first months of Elliot's life I managed to write the opening chapter of this book (the initial impetus was a request for a story for the anthology *Motherlove*), and I also cobbled together an application for an Australia Council Literature Board grant. It was not the best proposal I had ever produced, yet I was pleased that I had made the deadline before the close of applications.

After I sent the application off I was surprised by depression. Here I was, forty years old, four novels down the track, published in Australia, England, America and soon to be published in France, and I still couldn't manage to sell enough books in order to have a reasonable amount of money to live on.

In a good year I might earn $40,000 or even $50,000, but this usually represented two or even three years work, and my actual income was probably closer to $15,000. In the months after Elliot was born I had agreed to take up a writer-in-residency at a private boy's school in Brisbane later in the year, mainly because I needed the money.

I knew well enough that Les did not want to be shackled forever to the breadwinner's role, and I also knew that whenever my money ran out we began to fight. More than anything I wanted to be financially independent, yet the work I had chosen paid modestly.

In truth I felt like a failure applying for another grant. The contemptuous hiss of economic rationalism, in which a 'product's' intrinsic value is judged by how many people want to buy it, was sounding in my ears.

I think I was entering that dark wood of middle age, even before my body betrayed me.

Before I knew it, the momentous three month milestone had come and gone, and my breasts were still flowing with milk. One day, when Elliot was about three-and-a-half months old, I suddenly realised that the dreaded moment when my milk was supposed to dry up had already passed.

I was still stuffing cut-up nappies down my bra to mop up leaking milk, and Elliot was still feeding effortlessly.

It was as if I had broken the family curse.

It seemed to me that when I next ventured outdoors, on a long trip in the car to a place I no longer remember, the season had dramatically changed. I had delivered Elliot and spent most of the following weeks indoors, feeding and resting, lying naked on the bed because of the heat. Occasionally, when Les's parents were still down, I ventured out on a picnic, but quickly returned to the relative cool of the warehouse, feeling battered by hot wind and sun.

Now, driving through the boulevards of Melbourne, I saw that the trees had turned. The bright greens of summer had turned to browns, reds and golds, and drifts of dried leaves had settled on footpaths and roads. People were wearing light jumpers and long pants again.

Staring out the window of the car, I felt as if I had just woken from some timeless slumber. It seemed to me that I had been lying in our bedroom above the laneway for weeks, months, until I had lost track of days and seasons. When I entered the room it had been in the broil of summer, and yet my eyes were telling me that it was autumn and the world had been turning all the while.

Having a baby is like that: for a time you are truly absent from the outside world and from history. Elliot was born and the next thing I knew he was suddenly a dead weight to carry in my arms, and the earth had embarked on a new season.

He and I had been away, writing our own personal histories.

On a clear blue day in the middle of May, when Elliot was sixteen weeks old, I went to the toilet for a wee.

As I stood up and turned around to flush the toilet, I happened to glance down at my underpants. There, like a fine spray of sand, were microscopic specks of faeces.

Basically, shit was coming out my vagina.

12

The Purse So Deep

You'll find the Purse so deep,
You'll hardly come to the treasure.

FROM *A PLEASANT NEW*
BALLADE BEING A MERRY
DISCOURSE BETWEEN A
COUNTRY LASS AND
A YOUNG TAYLOR, C 1670.

In an article in London's *Observer*, Germaine Greer wrote that a vagina is no more internal than a nostril or an earhole. According to the vocabulary of penetration, she argued, one might as well claim that sticking one's little finger up someone's nose was 'entering' someone.

She seemed surprised that despite great advances in medical technology, and the subsequent assault on the mysteries of the body (and in particular the female body) which has resulted, the mystique of penetration has deepened and intensified.

According to Dr Greer this is largely because sex still has a penetration agenda, by which she means only intromission, or the putting of a penis inside a vagina, is considered the real thing (*pace* Bill and Monica). Only this singular act constitutes 'union', as the man 'entering' the woman.

She goes on to argue that as a result of this pervasive ideology all other sex acts (including foreplay) have been regarded as inferior to penetration in some 'far-reaching mystical way'.

By implication, Dr Greer lays the blame for this at the feet, so to speak, of the mighty penis. Because men have penises and because men still largely run the world, they are therefore still in control of the penetration agenda. In her words, men are still doing things to women rather than the other way around.

Furthermore, she complains that all that anyone wants to know about anyone these days is 'whose members got to penetrate them or who they penetrated with their members.'

But what if it is not the majestic penis after all which is setting the penetration agenda? What if it is instead that warm passage to the womb, the scented siren of the vagina, which keeps us viewing penetration in some far-reaching mystical way?

What if we still can't banish the mystery from our vaginas and wombs no matter how much we learn about the mechanics of reproduction, no matter how bright the light we shine on them, both literally and metaphorically?

I belong to the generation of women who were part of the assault on the mysteries of the female body. In my early twenties, when I worked as a volunteer counsellor for a feminist abortion referral clinic (and for a while afterwards), I sometimes referred to my vagina as my cunt.

I did this not to shock but to reclaim the word from men who used it in an ugly way against women, and to demystify the mythology which had grown up around the vagina. I believed in demystifying sex, in stripping it of its religious, spiritual and moral connotations and leaving instead a plain, honest bodily transaction.

I was and continue to be an admirer of Dr Greer's. Twenty or even ten years ago I would have agreed with her that a vagina is no more internal than a nostril or an earhole. Indeed, I accept that theoretically, still, the nostril and the earhole offer a pathway into the body in the same way that the vagina does, the only difference being where those pathways lead.

But, Dr Greer, I have to say that when the pathway into my womb began to be despoiled by shit, I no longer felt that pathway to be as neutral an entry point into my body as my nostril or earhole.

I felt it instead to be the entry to my very centre, where life had sparked within me. I felt that my own personal assault on demystifying sexual words and organs was rendered meaningless, and that the full power of my own body's essential mystery was revealed to me.

I felt completely and utterly defiled. I wanted the inviolate holiness of my vagina back.

*

As any self-respecting feminist who has inspected her own genitals knows, a healthy vagina is a self-cleaning organ, maintaining an easy balance between alkalines and acids, with fewer germs than the inside of a mouth. It is male fears which have imbued it with imaginary teeth, imaginary bad odours, with the ability to suck good men dry.

I had mostly treated mine with a certain nonchalance, for I had never suffered disease or even minor infections, and if I ever gave a thought to my vagina, it was probably to do with the concept of pleasure. I only knew I had a womb at all because I sometimes suffered appalling period pain, yet at the same time I could not quite believe that beneath my skin I carried internal organs.

I knew of course that they must be in there somewhere, doing whatever it was that insides did in order to keep one alive, yet I never gave a thought to the running of my body. My skin was the net in which the rest of me was caught, and my insides seemed as remote to me as the bottom of the ocean.

You might say that I took my vagina for granted, along with the rest of me, for when I was young I had that particular kind of dumb confidence in my body many lucky young women have.

I was not vain exactly, probably because I was conscious from the start of my chest bones marking me out as different from the norm. Also, I have always had the mixed blessing of knowing my own faults too well (both psychological and physical) and so I was always aware that the features of my face could not by any means be called beautiful.

I knew I had a cartoonish nose (my brothers used to joke that I didn't need needles to play records, all I had to do was lower my head and use my nose) and I saw that my teeth were not straight in my mouth. And yet, despite the scar on my chest and the hairy legs and the nose which could open tin cans, I felt easy in my net of skin.

Throughout my twenties I happily paraded my body on beaches and streets, and only sometimes remembered to hold my stomach in. I ate what I liked (and as a consequence was sometimes plump) and had the kind of broad-shouldered body and well-muscled legs which sometimes caused people to ask whether I was a dancer or a swimmer. I had the good fortune to look like someone who went to the gym even when I had never been inside one.

I blithely let numerous boys take photographs of me, and once, when I briefly shared a flat with a young newspaper photographer, I opened my red kimono wide and smiled as he photographed my small breasts. I still have the colour negative slides, and when I hold them up to the light I can see my young face and body graced by that thoughtless confidence.

As many young women do, I lived a life of the senses. When I was about twenty-four I impulsively left Sydney to live with a man who turned out to be a heavy drinker, and I remember hot days in Brisbane with sweat behind my knees and the particular sweet alcoholic scent which came from his soft, oily skin. We spent hours nestled together, like babies.

During this time I probably drank more than I ever have before or since, until I realised what I was doing. My body was the vessel in which I sailed, and I never once imagined it capsizing. If I drank too much my stomach simply heaved up its contents, my head ached for a while, and then I was righted again.

For a long time I ran at full sail, the wind roaring in my ears, heading for some endless horizon. My body seemed to steer itself and my vagina was along for the ride.

Among the many seminal (!) feminist texts on my bookshelf were the Boston Women's Health Collective *Our Bodies, Ourselves* and

Germaine Greer's *The Female Eunuch*. Both suggested all women
should be on friendly terms with their own vaginas, and Greer went
as far as declaring that if the idea of tasting your own menstrual
blood made you sick you still had a long way to go as an emanci-
pated woman.

While I have never gathered in a circle on the floor with my best
women friends while we inspected each other's vaginas with a
speculum (described as empowering in *Our Bodies, Ourselves*), I
believed that knowledge was power. Unlike my grandmother and
mother before me, by the age of twenty-one I knew precisely where
all the various components of my sexual organs were located, and
exactly what they were for.

Before herpes, before AIDS, before sex became another dispos-
able consumer item in a market-driven culture, my friends and I
believed in the free use of our bodies. Our sexual organs were like
sweets of the body, made for pleasure, and we gave no thought
whatsoever to nutritional value.

Ours was the first generation of women in human history able to
disconnect sex from reproduction. The pill represented the scissors
in our hands and we cut away gladly, never doubting the wisdom of
severing that link, both actual and symbolic, never considering the
question of whether at the same time we might also be banishing the
divine from the house of love.

Hidden in my skin my vagina folded in on itself, opening like a
flower when pleasured. Its plump, glistening crevices led to the neck
of my womb, where my cervix rested. When I touched my cervix
with a finger it felt like the tip of my nose.

Before I left London, when I was first pregnant with Caspar, I
watched a television documentary in which a tiny camera nestling

in a woman's vagina filmed her orgasm. Astonishingly, at the moment of orgasm the cervix sat up and dipped like the beak of a bird into a pool of semen. It was actively gathering the possibility of life into itself.

My own cervix has performed that feat, my own vagina has enfolded the penis of the father of my children and, as if Gods, we created new life.

In delivering up my babies my vagina once had the magnitude and burn of the stars.

Within days of discovering the faecal soiling, a date for the repair operation was set. The Professor assured me that no further damage could be done within this short time, and the only consideration in the days before I entered hospital was personal hygiene.

I took to having several showers a day, hopping in before a breast feed, before Les got home, after I went to the toilet. Even though the so-called soiling was infinitesimal, I could not recover from the shock of it, the feeling that what was happening to my body was a perversion.

At some point during those anxious waiting days before I went into hospital, Les and I began to turn away from each other.

I only learnt later that it wasn't because I repulsed him (as I feared), but that I was somehow travelling to a place where he could not go. It was as if we could no longer quite catch the sound of each other's voices.

Neither of us knew then how long it would be, or how far I would have to go without him.

In the days before I went into hospital, I began collecting information. I rang the Nursing Mothers Association, the hospital lactation consultant, and various doctors, asking about the effect the drugs would have on my breastmilk and therefore on Elliot's body. I was relieved to discover the risk was negligible.

I learned, too, that the procedure itself had a success rate of over ninety per cent, and little by little I began to lose my fear. In fact I surprised myself by beginning to look forward to going into hospital.

Of course, what I was looking forward to was getting rid of the faecal soiling, of my sense of being despoiled, and to waking up one morning without a fistula. Before long, though, I also started to relish the idea of hospital as a place where I would be able to rest and let someone else do the cooking, cleaning and washing.

When the time came to pack my bags I was positively excited, as if I were going on holiday and the only thing I had to fear was sunburn.

I remember the afternoon I checked in, how surprised I was at the luxury of the private room. It hardly looked different to a mid-priced hotel, with a double bed and decent prints, tasteful carpets and an ensuite bathroom. As I placed Elliot in the specially provided cot and unpacked my things, happiness swelled within me.

It is a feature of my personality that I am often able to find a sense of joy and adventure in unlikely places and things. Along with my ability to see the worst in my own character and to be consequently plunged into despair, I am frequently saved from my own worst self by the chance glance of sunlight through a window, a sweet remark, a wonderful burst of flavour in my mouth.

Lest I appear a simpleton, I should assure you that these moments of grace are exactly that, and I am as capable as the next person of spending whole days and weeks without light. Yet I am frequently visited by happiness, and am always grateful for such moments. Even as I entered that dark wood I still sensed light.

When the Professor's assistant came to explain the procedure again, reiterating its high success rate but informing me of what could go wrong, as he was obliged to do by law, I signed the permission form with only the briefest of hesitations.

When the assistant left I opened the blinds wide and smiled out the window. I still had doubts, but I also had a large dash of hope. There was more than a ninety per cent chance I was going to wake up from the anaesthetic without a fistula.

Later that night, after all the nurses had come in to coo at Elliot and ask if they could hold him, I walked around the corridors of the ward because I could not sleep. I was suddenly sober once more, frightened even, remembering everything that had gone wrong already. I reminded myself too that I was on the oncology ward, or the cancer ward to dispense with the euphemism, and that the room I was in was probably so pleasant because it was a room where seriously ill women battled death.

As I walked down the corridor I saw sick women with bedside lamps still burning, perhaps trying to read and distract themselves from that discourse being held deep in their bodies to which they could not speak directly. I wondered about those women who did not have their lights on, if they were lying in the dark visualising their cancers being attacked by healthy cells, if they were somehow trying to get a word in edgeways in that faraway discourse.

I tried to claim back my old feeling of luck, telling myself that at least I did not have cancer. I had a relatively minor problem with my body's mechanics, and compared with what I could have wrong it was a form of self-indulgence to feel frightened.

I turned around and headed back to my room, in order to be comforted by the living breath of my sleeping baby.

13
Whatever's at Hand

Let me go down on your carpet,
your straw mattress — whatever's at hand
because the child in me is dying, dying.

ANNE SEXTON,
THE BREAST

Do I need to remind you here that my actual waking life runs beneath these words like an underground river? That Les and I are partners in a secret, as all marriages are? Should I tell you that as I have been writing this Les and I found the weight of what we carried too much to bear, and after one calamitous day we found ourselves living apart?

All the while I have been writing, my story has been uncurling. Like your own, my story is still being told, and I am living the telling as I write it, breathing, trusting in the dark.

I am writing backwards but I am living forwards, blind to my own end.

The day of the operation I woke up in the recovery room with my teeth chattering. 'Are you cold, Susan?' a nurse wearing a face mask asked, and I nodded. I didn't know where I was, what the time was, whether I had already had the operation. I woke up again when someone wrapped me in what appeared to be baking foil or some kind of space blanket for astronauts.

Someone was taking my pulse, I was aware of fussing around me. At different times I heard the beep of electrical equipment, a voice on the radio, nurses talking about something I could not understand. I could not feel my body.

The next thing I knew I was being rolled off a trolley and onto a bed, and another nurse was telling me I was back in the ward, next door to the room I was in before. 'You'll be in here for a day or two so we can keep an eye on you, then you can go back to your room.'

'Where's my baby?' I asked. 'Where's Elliot?'

'Your mum's looking after him. He's next door, I think.'

I was tired of concentrating. I fell asleep.

I drifted in and out of consciousness until I heard the sound of Elliot's voice. 'Here she is, here's your lovely Mummy,' said my mother, handing him to me. With some difficulty I rolled over on my side and straight away he opened his mouth blindly for the nipple.

He was whole, all of a piece, a seamless creation. I held him to me and for a moment the beat of pain within me was stilled.

I had expressed some milk before the operation, in case I was too sick to feed. I found instead that I craved the honest suck of Elliot's working mouth, the sense that he was making my body do its proper job.

I remembered describing to a friend a few days before the operation the precise details of what was going to happen. 'But that's genital mutilation!' she cried, as if offended on my behalf.

I lay on the bed, bleeding, willingly mutilated, with drips sticky-taped to the back of my hand, and felt only gladness that some part of my body was still able to go about its business, oblivious to the wreckage below.

That first night I lay as if pinned to the bed by pain, the throb between my legs radiating up and out until it seemed to reach the tips of my fingers. I was in the half dark and my genitals were turning purple, a great dark bruising covering them like a blush. A nurse was sitting on a chair beside the bed, telling me an endless story about how her first marriage had gone wrong, and only my habitual politeness kept me from screaming at her to shut up.

Moreover, my own mouth seemed to be producing sounds of

empathy, sentences about the perfidiousness of certain types of men. Pain was stamping within me, counting out its particular beat, and I was still trying to be a nice girl.

Do some nurses lose their sensitivity paradoxically *because* of their overwhelming intimacy with human pain and loss? Do some ears lose their hearing, some eyes lose their capacity to notice? Or are some people born with an innate ability to withstand the sight of the body's breakdown, revealing the right personality for nursing in the first place?

A sensitive nurse is your agent, acting as your own body at its best, walking for you, plumping up your pillows, rearranging your own useless limbs. A sensitive nurse has her ear to your heart and understands the dependability of pain and its attendant sorrows, its sneaky embrace of your body and mind.

For of course it is not only your bruised centre that is feeling the pain but your mind's notion of your former seamless self. You are the witness to your own decline, the sole occupant of the body now under attack.

A sensitive nurse understands this to be a profoundly lonely experience.

The Professor was pleased with how the operation went. 'Everything's looking good,' he said the next morning on his rounds. 'How's the pain?'

'Not too bad,' I said and it wasn't by then, for post-operative pain is an odd thing, hiding within, lying low as if to gather strength for the next assault.

'You're looking well, anyway,' he said, smiling as he went out the door surrounded by his team.

Out of self-defence, every nurse and every doctor in the medical profession must necessarily divide the person from the patient. How else could one poor nurse or one poor doctor go on, bearing the weight of human tears and sorrows?

The sensitive nurses and doctors (and the Professor was certainly one) are those who remember that they once made the division, and that tied to the patient is a living person, twinned to her body's distress.

How to explain that my body kept producing milk, throughout this and the traumas to follow? That my anxiety, my fears, my depressions and all the drugs coursing through me didn't cause my milk to curdle? I wouldn't have been surprised to find my nipples oozing blood, but they continued to produce thin, nutritious milk.

My continued milk production became symbolic to me, a supply line of hope to the future.

On his visits to the hospital Caspar enjoyed sitting next to me on the bed, operating the remote control television set in the ceiling. He also enjoyed pressing the buzzer for the nurse, making the bed go up and down, eating the little biscuits in plastic packets I saved for him. Within minutes he successfully wrought chaos.

Of necessity his visits were kept short, and in truth I was often relieved to see him go. He always wanted to be up on the bed (to play with all the electrical devices rather than to be close to me) and consequently I was usually trampled. The hospital was an exciting place for him, and he was generally happy to be ushered out the door towards the thrill of the elevator.

I was feeling well, back in my luxurious carpeted room, getting ready for my first post-operative poo. When the great moment came

I was ushered into the ensuite bathroom, conscious of the waiting audience.

I was so worried about disturbing the stitches I could hardly bear to sit on the toilet seat. I had already looked in a mirror and seen that my diminished perineum had been completely repaired and that there was an unbroken line of stitches running from my vagina to my anus. Half-standing, half-sitting, I waited for the searing pain I was sure would come.

To my great surprise I felt only mildly uncomfortable. When I emerged from the bathroom to give the good news to my audience I felt as if I had successfully played Carnegie Hall.

When it was clear there was no further faecal soiling following my visit to the toilet (do I really have to tell you all this?) the Professor and his team seemed to think this was a good indication that the fistula had finally been conquered. I was allowed home.

The stitches were painful, and friends suggested rubber rings, salt baths, healing oils. I had two baths a day, and walked around as if I had just given birth to an elephant. Sitting down was excruciating and the mere act of lowering myself into a chair and standing up again seemed insurmountable.

But I was happy and felt as if I had been given back my life. My mother began to pack her bags for her return flight, and we began to prepare to resume the shape of an ordinary family. Les was still sleeping downstairs on the futon, but we were both looking forward to finding an alternative solution for Caspar's nocturnal roaming and to Les's reclamation of the marital bed.

*

The morning my mother was due to fly home I went to the toilet. I was constipated (despite the gallons of water and endless pieces of fruit) yet I resisted straining. I stood up from the seat once or twice, sat down again, finally managing to do the business.

The skin between my legs suddenly felt peculiar, stretched too tight, as if something beneath the skin was being pulled to breaking point.

'Oh, it's just your imagination,' said my mother reassuringly. 'Why don't you give the doctor a ring if you're worried?'

Les already believed I worried too much, and I dared not say anything to him.

I took a mirror upstairs and lay back on the bed. It looked to me as if the stitches were coming loose: I did not know if they were meant to dissolve, if this was how they were supposed to look.

I jumped up and ran downstairs to my mother. 'I think the stitches are coming apart!' I said, beginning to cry.

'Ring the doctor,' she said. 'I'm sure it's all right.'

I remember it was Friday morning and the Professor returned my call just after Mum had left for the airport. She seemed to think I was panicking, and that I just needed reassurance, but told me to ring her anyway after I had spoken to the doctor.

I described to the Professor the strange sensations I was experiencing, my fears that the stitches appeared to be pulling or coming loose or doing something distinctly odd.

'Why don't we wait and see what happens over the next few days,' he said. 'It would be unusual for anything to go wrong at this stage. What are we — ten days down the track? It's unlikely anything will happen now.'

I made no response. 'Well, Susan, you know your own perineum. If you think there's a problem, then I'll be happy to see you and examine you. Come in and see me on Monday.'

'And what happens if the repair is breaking down? What then?'

'Oh, I wouldn't worry about that yet,' he replied.

'I want to know,' I insisted.

'We usually do a temporary colostomy to divert the faeces and allow the area to heal. A good proportion of fistulas spontaneously heal themselves once there's no faeces passing through.'

After thanking him I hung up, alone in the kitchen, Elliot asleep upstairs.

I wanted to lie down forever and never risk movement again.

How do I tell you about lying awake alone in the bed the next night, having discovered my flesh coming apart like rotten fruit, and knowing that it meant a colostomy? How do I transmit to you the fear in my cells, the feeling that my own body was splitting like two halves of a peach? This was the night I left the desperate message on the Professor's private telephone, the night I felt panic scrambling in the cage of my chest. I feared that the wall of flesh between my vagina and my anus was breaking down, and that by morning I would be left with only one passage out of my lower body, my body's waste cradled in the folds of my vagina.

I lay on the bed and a sound like a howl escaped me. I have heard this sound only one other time in my life, when my mother was told her oldest friend was weeks or even days away from dying.

It is the sound of life shrieking at death. It is the monstrous sound of grief, of furious denial.

Do you want me to describe the picture that next morning of myself and Les? Do you want to see me in that large cavernous warehouse, sobbing in my pink dressing gown, while Les tried to calm me down? Les's form of reassurance, is the male way of reassurance, and he kept saying, 'Wait till the Professor examines you, Susan. You won't know for sure till then.'

He was trying to extract the panic from the situation, he was trying to make everything go away. 'Les! Les! The stitches are coming apart! I'll have to have a colostomy!' I finally screamed at him, clawing my way towards his chest.

In this picture you will be able to see all the other pictures that were to follow: Susan gets emotional, Les gets rational, consequently Susan feels she is not being heard or supported and Les feels he spends his entire bloody life mopping up Susan's anxieties.

In other words the paint had already dried on us. Both of us felt trapped in the frame.

How do you get the will to pack your bags to go back into hospital when you have only just emerged victorious? This time there was no excitement in me, no sense of adventure, only the slow, steady pump of fear as I got ready to go.

The only thing that made me hang on was knowing that my mother would be back.

Inside I was three years old, waiting for my mother to magically make everything all right.

When I was a girl and got frightened of a scary man or a scary situation on the television, my grandmother, whom I loved desperately (and still do), used to say, 'Don't worry, sweetie, it's only a movie.' Often she simply turned the television off.

It was her way of reassuring me. She was, and is, a woman who dwells in the light, refusing to acknowledge the dark. In her late seventies, when I was still living in Paris, she found a lump in her breast, and I remember sleepless nights worrying about her, wondering how I found myself so far away.

When I called Australia to find out the test results she told me everything was fine. 'I never once thought it was cancer, Susie,' she said. 'I'm not the type.'

I thought of my grandmother the morning I was due to go into hospital to have a temporary colostomy, and tried to summon some of her light. But my thoughts kept veering towards the shadows, and I could not quiet the dark bird of panic flailing within me. I found myself thinking: *what if real life turns more catastrophic than a movie, Nan? What happens when there is no button to turn off?*

Les brought me some English newspapers to take into hospital, but I could not concentrate on them. My eye was caught by a photograph in a glossy Sunday magazine supplement: black slimy saltwater eels ready for the cooking pot. They lay glistening as if with mucus, entwined in a grotesque embrace, and as soon as my eye chanced upon them I slammed the magazine shut.

The dark slime of the eels was like my own dank, malodorous intestines, swimming within me, about to be hauled to the light.

I did not know what a colostomy was, but thought it involved tubes, plastic bags, drainage holes. I envisaged a kind of permanent intravenous tube line I would have to pull around wherever I went, like a leper ringing her bell.

Actually, I didn't think much at all. My mind simply shut down after a certain point, and I stopped asking questions. I did wonder, though, if I could cope with what was about to happen to me, if I had the particular kind of strength needed to carry on.

I knew I was not like my grandmother: I am the type of woman who on finding a lump in her breast immediately thinks of cancer. Also, my job as a writer is to shun the light and actively go forth into shadow, to shine my puny torch into darkened spaces, upon that which I would rather not know or acknowledge.

The torch was in my hand but I could not bear to look. I did not want to open my eyes to reality.

14
Inside Out

'I am DISINTEGRATION.'

FRIDA KAHLO
WORDS ON A SELF-PORTRAIT,
1953

On the afternoon of Wednesday, June 11, 1997 my mother walked into my hospital room and I collapsed, sobbing. Like a child I wanted only my mother, not my husband or even my baby sons, only her. Beneath my hard tears, my flailing panic, I was shocked at the fierceness of my emotions, at how like a suffering child I felt. The whole time I had been lying in bed waiting for the wardsmen to come and take me to theatre I had been trying to compose a kind of speech to my mother, in which I meant to apologise for all the grief I had caused her and to tell her how much I loved her. I could not believe the vastness of the love I had unearthed, how abandoned and frightened I felt without her.

When she finally walked into the room my mouth immediately crumpled and my speaking voice turned into a sob. As she rushed towards me, words strangled in my throat and she shushed me and told me gently not to bother speaking. 'No, no, Mum,' I said, trying to talk through my crying, 'I need to say this ... you must have mothered me very well for me to feel safe when you are here. I've been waiting for you ... only for you ...' I could not go on.

She started to blink and then a nurse walked in and the swollen moment was gone.

The word colostomy is derived from Greek: 'kolon' which means large bowel, 'stoumon' which means to provide an opening, and 'tome' which means a cutting operation.

A colostomy is your large bowel brought to the surface of your skin, cut open.

Before the wardsmen came to take me to theatre, the hospital therapist responsible for new mastectomy patients and new colostomy patients came to see me. She wore bright red lipstick and purple and pink floating garments; her high heels clicked across the linoleum. Her job was to reassure me, to demonstrate the efficacy of a modern colostomy bag, to stop me from jumping out the window.

As you would expect, her manner was calm and sympathetic. After we had talked for a while she gave a kind of colostomy show, displaying photographs of tiny babies with colostomy bags, demonstrating what a bag looked like and how it was attached to the body, assuring me it was both leakproof and odourless.

She insisted I would be just the same as everybody else after the colostomy, except that where I passed faeces from was a couple of inches higher up.

So I would not get too much of a shock when I first looked at my stomach after the operation, she told me my exposed bowel was called a 'stoma' and would protrude perhaps half an inch above my skin.

She pulled down her bottom lip. 'It'll look a bit like the lining of your lower lip, shiny and dark pink. For the first few days you'll have a plastic clip passing underneath it to hold it in place and you'll see the stitches where it's been sewn to the abdominal wall.'

I noticed her hair looked as if it had been recently cut, she wore it short, feathered around her ears, and her eyelashes were thick with mascara. I wondered how much older she was than me.

There was a knock on the door and a sweet-voiced Irish woman came in, out of nursing uniform like the therapist, apologising for interrupting. The therapist motioned her over and introduced her as a trainee stomal therapist from a country hospital. 'Do you mind if she sits in?'

'Not at all,' I said, for a woman who is about to have her bowel exposed must learn to grow accustomed to exposure.

'You poor dear,' the trainee therapist said in her soft curly tongue. 'What an outcome from having one little baby.'

She patted my arm and my eyes clouded; I lay back on the pillow.
'Oh, well,' I said, my eyes closed, 'it could be worse. I am on the
cancer ward after all. At least I'm not dying.'

I heard the hospital therapist's voice. 'All the ladies compare
themselves on this ward,' she was telling the trainee. 'It happens all
the time.'

When I opened my eyes the trainee's face was full of sadness.

It is a disgusting failure of privacy. Like an exposed liver.

Amy Witting, *I For Isobel*

A colostomy pouch is about the size of a pappadum or a small,
round pocket pitta bread. At the top a hole is cut around the stoma
and a kind of superior bandaid keeps this area stuck to the belly
while the actual bag hangs away from the body. There are no tubes,
drainage lines, or attachments. It usually only 'works' once a day,
and for the rest of the time the pouch hangs empty.

The stoma lying beneath the pouch has no nerve endings and,
consequently, no sensation.

The hospital therapist was telling me my life would go on as before
and, with luck, I would only have the temporary colostomy for a
matter of months. 'You'll still be able to ski, swim, do everything
you did before,' she went on. 'If you like I'll see if _____, another
young colostomate, can come and talk to you. She wears mini skirts
up to here and it's never bothered her.'

Groovy, I can't wait, I thought, *a colostomy bag as fashion
statement!*

*

When she thought I was ready, the hospital therapist took a black marker pen from her colostomy show kit and asked me to get up from the bed. 'I'm going to position your stoma now,' she said, 'would you mind slipping your nightie off?'

She looked at me standing in my underpants for what seemed to me a long time. 'Do you wear jeans?' she asked and I nodded. 'I'm just looking for the best place to put it,' she said, 'we don't want it too high on your waist.'

I was being fitted for my own bowel, a new form of body decoration. Finally she drew a large black cross on my stomach, to the left of my belly button, and then heavily circled the cross. 'Looks like a No Smoking sign, doesn't it?' she joked.

I thought: *ha bloody ha.*

Once an English friend in Paris made me furious by declaring that suffering revealed a person's true character. At the time I was dumb with grief over the break-up of my first marriage, and I suppose she was trying to tell me to stiffen my spine and show the world what I was made of. I remember thinking mean-spirited thoughts about her. I thought: *just you wait till your own nightmare wakes, loud and roaring, just wait till it comes alive to scream in your face.*

I am living proof that suffering does not ennoble character. At least initially, suffering only makes you cross with everyone, angry at the world.

Fresh suffering makes you hate jesting therapists, it makes you cry while you wait to go into an operating theatre to have your bowel cut open.

Fresh suffering makes you ask: *whatever made me think I could have a baby without consequence like everybody else?*

*

In the waiting room for the operating theatre a kind nurse was trying to make us smile by asking if we were wearing any sexy underwear under our operating gowns. There were old women, young women, Caucasians, Chinese, lying naked under flimsy operating garments, on our backs staring up at the ceiling. We were waiting to have cancerous breasts removed, waiting while wedding rings were taped to our fingers, waiting to find out if the cancers in our uteruses had been tamed. Our hair was covered by paper operating caps.

The therapist who had earlier drawn the target upon my skin was trying to have a conversation about football with a young Chinese breast cancer patient who didn't speak much English. She was being jolly, joking with the other nurses about the respective merits of Australian Rules teams, doing her best to cheer the frightened young woman about to undergo a mastectomy.

The fear in the room was manifest in the pained silences, in the throat clearings and last minute requests to use the toilet. A hefty, sixtyish Italian woman tried to get off the trolley she was on without exposing her naked backside (the gowns were loosely tied at the back), and I had to turn away from her distress. She was red in the face, smiling with clumsy embarrassment.

When I turned my face to the side, a tear escaped from my eye and slid slowly to the sheet.

A hideous accidie — *the kind of despair that breeds hell's climate* — *overwhelmed me* ... I must be wicked to deserve such pain *is the predominant burden.*
                              Rosamond Lehmann, *The Swan in the Evening*

*

When I woke up I did not want to look at my stomach. I opened my eyes and stared up at nothing. I had tubes in my hands and back. I could not feel the lower half of my body because I had been given a spinal epidural for pain relief.

I did not feel anything. I did not feel anything.

Did Les come into the room? Did my mother? I was absent on the pillow, I could not move my legs. Once I lifted the sheet and looked down at my dead legs beneath the epidural, white, bloated, like a dead woman's. A nurse re-arranged them for me, lifting them like unconscious animals.

I thought: *How tired I am of everything.*

A young anaesthetist came to top up the epidural. He lifted me up and I leaned forward while he injected fresh drugs into the tube taped to my lower spine.

The drug rose up in me like a wave, drowning me so that my lungs seemed filled with water and I feared they would not inflate again. A paralysis was creeping up my body, like fouled water.

'Keep breathing,' the nurse said.

I had to look because I had to wash the slough off the wound. I had to learn to clean myself, to become skilled at certain necessary manoeuvres before I left hospital.

I had to look.

Friday, June 12? 13?

My new rosy anus
my sprouting rose
my stomach arsehole
blooming

All the while this was going on I was writing in my red and black notebook. I was writing to save my life, to keep myself breathing, to reclaim some illusory sense of control. My handwriting was larger than normal, pressed hard into the page, and this is the moment where I discovered that writing can be a way of escaping pain, a pushing away, a means of putting distance between myself and reality.

I always thought writing was exposure, a peeling back, but I think now perhaps it can also be a covering up, a pasting over of wounds. For the first time I am conscious that writing can also be a distancing device. I always thought it was a process by which I brought everything closer, made everything more real, more pinned down, more mine, but now I see it is also a way of putting some safe distance, some order, some SPACE between myself and my real life. While all this is happening to me I am recording myself as a way of stepping outside the reality of having a bag of shit stuck to my belly. I am aware, self-conscious, my own comfort ...

Have I mentioned that I kept on feeding Elliot? That all through the violence being inflicted upon my body, the degradation, the indignity, the disintegration of my previous known self, my breasts continued their heavenly pump?

Have I mentioned that Elliot lay beside me on the bed, oblivious to shit and blood, untouched by knives?

How dumb to life men's bodies seemed to me, how insensible, how untrammelled. They struck me as locked up, impenetrable, all of a piece, *unbloodied*. I suddenly saw why men feared women's bodies so, the blood and mucus and guts of us, the leakiness of us, the *seep* of us, able to be entered into, inhabited, changed utterly.

Men's bodies go on essentially unchanged, decaying, freezing over, petrifying in their original state, a slow petrifying process, like trees.

Women's bodies fill with babies' legs and arms, teeming with life, women's bodies rot, burst open, come apart at the seams.

Like me, like me.

Both times I was pregnant my sole focus was on the baby. Will he be delivered to us whole? Alive? Even during my second pregnancy with Elliot, knowing I had a fistula, I never gave much thought to my own health beyond worrying about management of the actual birth, about a vaginal versus a caesarean delivery.

I never once considered it might be myself whose body was capsized.

> *The sadness of life takes hold of people as best it may, but it seems almost always to manage to take hold of them somehow …*
>
> Celine, *Journey to the End of the Night*

Do you want to see the volunteer craft woman come into the room and ask me if I wanted to join the other ladies for a craft morning? Do you want to see me refusing to accept my fate, raging at the failure of my corporeal self? Do you want to see me grit my teeth so I do not let the howl escape me for a second time?

On my first day standing up my legs wobbled like a newborn foal. Aided by a nurse I walked a couple of steps to the bathroom.

'Do you want your make-up?' she asked.

I did not want to adorn myself in any manner. I did not want to admit that other people existed to look upon me.

I did not want to leave hospital.

On my first tentative walk around the ward corridors I was introduced to the other new colostomy patient, a young woman from country Victoria, who had a cancerous growth in her womb. She had been on the IVF program when it had been discovered. She was talkative and cracked black jokes, flipping aside her dressing gown to show me her new colostomy bag. 'Look at me, eh,' she said. 'No baby and cancer of the womb.' She asked if she could come around to my room later to see Elliot.

I walked slowly back, thinking of a womb sprouting death, of a cancerous placenta. I was conscious of having crossed some line, of having entered a new country inhabited by the old, the sick and the dying.

Outside the hospital windows men and women walked the streets, but I knew that even when I was returned to them I would no longer be the same as before.

*

My exposed bowel resembled a map of Australia made up of human organs. When the plastic clip holding it up was removed, it contracted to the shape of a fifty cent piece. With the plastic clip gone my captured bowel did not slip back into my body as I thought it might but stood up from my stomach, a tiny flesh hill.

Frequently during the long days which followed, obscene images passed through my mind: myself eating a bowl of soup in which stomas floated on the scummy surface, like turds.

The large bowel has no muscle in it and therefore no muscle control. You cannot pass faeces at will, you cannot prevent the sound of wind escaping.

One morning a loud fart came from the stoma. The nurse in the room laughed and said, 'Oh dear, excuse you!' Tears sprang up in my eyes.

'You can always blame it on the baby, love,' she said by way of comfort, 'and if you don't have him with you, quickly look around as if it was someone else.'

She was still chuckling at her own wit as she left the room.

Elliot attracted everyone: nurses, cleaners, administrative assistants, women with intrusive cancers eating up their bodies and their lives, all drawn by the freight of hope babies carry. He lay back in his cot playing blissfully with his toes or sucked mindlessly on a mirror next to me in bed. One nurse begged to take him for a walk around the ward, so other nurses could coo around his pram.

Perhaps because Elliot was oblivious to table manners and other adult customs, everyone who came into my room seemed relaxed, a little unwrapped. A cleaner held his finger while she told me it took her two hours to get into work every morning, how she got up at four in a distant suburb to get to work by six thirty. She thought that was probably the reason why she and her husband had never been able to have children, because her body was always too tired.

Other nurses, young, optimistic, told me about their lives in inner city suburbs, about old boyfriends from Geelong. In this way, by doing nothing more active than lying in my bed, I learnt about the spatial and emotional distance between Melbourne and Geelong, the entanglements between them, about Geelong girls who gravitate to the city.

In a strange, unexpected way, the city I had lived in for two-and-a-half years but had never really come to know was finally being mapped for me, for every story brought to my bed was a lesson of sorts in personal geography.

In the years I had lived in Melbourne I had lived as if hemmed in by sea, only ever walking the same few streets, the same parks.

Without my active participation, the city was suddenly revealed to me, more vividly than any map.

The stomal therapist with the colourful clothes wanted to talk to me about my husband before I left hospital. Was I going to show him my stoma? In her experience husbands reacted very well to viewing the disaster area, with most saying something anti-climactic, like 'Oh, is that all it is?'

She felt that overall it was preferable that partners know exactly what was involved, lest either party get a shock should one unexpectedly walk in on the other.

Immediately I thought of horror movies, where the one who is a werewolf or an alien goes into another room to metamorphose, and the unsuspecting partner walks in. I saw myself peeling off my skin and Les opening the door to my boiled, skinless head.

I could not bear the thought of Les seeing my exposed bowel. I thought: *what happened to your old belief that knowledge equals power, Susan? What happened to your old belief that revealed secrets lose their power to harm?*

Les and I had one brief conversation about the matter. I dutifully reported to him the therapist's advice that both partners were supposed to feel relieved and more accepting of the situation if they knew exactly what was involved.

'Would you like to see it?' I asked, not looking at him.

'Not really,' he replied.

We did not speak of it again.

One night as I was trying to read in bed, Maryann from the book club walked unannounced into the room. Immediately my body clenched and went into a kind of red alert: my heart crashed in my chest, my hands began to sweat, every nerve, every part of me was focused on the colostomy. I had not told anyone outside my immediate family about the colostomy, and I feared it would announce itself catastrophically, exploding in some dreadful noise.

She was carrying an armful of beautiful scented flowers and I tried to concentrate on what she was saying. I wondered if my body's panic would induce some kind of internal convulsion, if shit would spray volcanically into my new bag.

Sensing my distress she did not stay long, and only when she had gone and I realised that my first encounter with the outside world had passed without incident did I reflect on her kindness.

Les had tried to warn her off visiting, but she had come anyway.

I was glad and for the first time I sensed a stepping stone back into life.

The night before I left hospital I dreamt I passed my seventeen-year-old self in the street. My seventeen-year-old self appeared to be leading some kind of procession through the city, I was wearing my old school uniform and I seemed full of glory, as if secretly convinced my coming life was going to be incandescent.

My forty-year-old self was going by in a car, I think, and I tried to attract the attention of my seventeen-year-old self, but I could not. She continued to walk smilingly ahead and she looked so confident, so happy, so thrilled with herself, that I was filled with an aching poignancy, and a fierce wish to protect her.

In the dream I was conscious that my forty-year-old self did not want to go back, to be her again, only that I felt a keen sadness.

I knew I would never be able to reach her.

15

Incidental Envelope

Uproot from the past, begin afresh. I will take you where you belong.

GOD TO ABRAHAM

It was just my luck that my particular birth complication involved poo. I mean, I couldn't have had a ladylike collapse of the kidneys through blood loss at the moment of birth, or suffered a demure little bout of pre-eclampsia. Oh no, my birth trauma had to concern bowels, didn't it, the body's waste, the great unmentionable. During my convalescence I clipped from a newspaper a story about screening for bowel cancer, which featured a frustrated doctor's lament about getting people to do anything about it. He said the time had come to ask ourselves why people weren't talking about bowel cancer. 'It's something to do with the dunny, isn't it? It's at the wrong end of things.'

To my closest friends who knew about the colostomy there must surely have been a delicious moment in which they savoured the irony of me having to admit that I shit at all. I come from a family which prefers to ignore the fact that humans pass waste, a family whose members will check out the distance of the toilet from the rest of the house before even considering an overnight invitation.

As houseguests some of us have been known to wake at five a.m., before anyone else is up, to ensure that we can make our shameful donations to some faraway sea in secrecy. Some of us carry personal bottles of toilet deodoriser when we travel, in case our host does not stock it, lest the smell of our shit reach somebody else's nostrils.

I myself have been known to avoid the toilets of friends and lovers altogether, to hang on until I reach the safety of a public toilet. A certain member of my family did not move his bowels once for four whole days when staying with friends, and consequently found himself severely constipated for weeks afterwards. A younger member of our family refused to use the toilets at school because of the terrible sound of 'plop'.

As you might imagine, I have never found jokes featuring farting amusing. I once had a boyfriend whose repertoire of jokes included references to incontinence and colostomy bags, and I rarely found them funny either. I remember reading a restaurant review in a London newspaper in which the reviewer spoke of obsequious waiters. 'Wine, sir? More water perhaps? Change your colostomy bag?' I found this tasteless even when I didn't have a colostomy myself.

Funny isn't it, Miss Anal Retentive, forced to consider her bowels. Isn't there a sense of divine irony in this, that some of us are forced to deal with the very thing of which we are most embarrassed?

When I got home I did not want to go out again. I did not yet know the intimate details of my body decoration, whether I could trust it when I went out in public. Besides, I was tired, tired to my very centre, broken.

It seemed to me that the world was in winter and the warehouse was always dark, and I could not find my way forward. I ate small, tentative meals, lost weight by the day, could not locate the right words to say to Les. I felt abandoned, alive without comfort, in need of nurture. Les appeared to be looking straight ahead, never meeting my eye, gone from me.

In those first weeks at home I cancelled the creative writing job at the boys' school in Brisbane and tried to shut down my fears of what would happen when my money ran out. I knew of course that Les would support me up to a certain point, but I also knew he had strong feelings about having to personally subsidise my writing because the publishing industry would not. He did not think it was fair that I continued to work at a job which brought in so little money, leaving him with no choices of his own.

At the end of the month we impulsively decided to sell the warehouse: it was too noisy, too dark, too unsuitable.

I knew of course that it was not our place of abode from which we wished to escape.

I rang the obstetrician I had originally consulted over the fistula to get her opinion on whether or not I should continue breastfeeding. She said that of course the final decision was up to me, but that there was some evidence that the hormonal changes resulting in giving up breastfeeding would be beneficial to my vagina spontaneously healing. She seemed to think the damaged area around the fistula might have a better chance once my vagina was fully oestrogenised.

You know, of course, that I had never had a problem feeding Elliot. Astonishingly, right up until this moment my breasts remained full of milk. I had fought and fought to keep feeding Caspar on a diminished milk supply, and now I found myself in the opposite situation, brimming with milk yet having to give breastfeeding up.

After I hung up the phone, I immediately rang the Maternal and Child Health help line. I found myself crying and the voice in my ear was saying something about my son not thanking me in twenty years time for continuing to breastfeed him if I was permanently incapacitated in some way.

I felt I had to stop breastfeeding, to give my body its best chance.

That same night I opened Elliot's first tin of formula.

He refused to drink it.

One morning Tracey came over to take me to the hairdresser's, amongst other things. My mother was still down, and we talked about Tracey's mother, June, who was my mother's oldest friend.

June was sick in Brisbane, suffering a mysterious affliction that had the doctors puzzled: problems with her balance, odd pains which came and went.

June's was a vivid personality, dramatic, passionate, and we laughed about her soon sorting those doctors out. I had once lived with the Callanders as a teenager while finishing a semester of school, and the whole family had always seemed to me like a family in a play, as if they lived their whole lives on a brightly lit stage. They were large and handsome, theatrical, big talkers with large ideas, and that morning just thinking about June caused my heart to lift momentarily.

With Tracey holding my arm, we walked together down the street, and I felt stiff with self-consciousness. It was the first time I had been out since I had left the hospital, and I had to remind myself to walk normally. It seemed to me that people looked at us oddly.

Thankfully, the hairdresser was also a friend, and I was relieved to see there would just be the three of us in the salon. Tracey perched up on the bench while Libby wielded her scissors.

The radio was on and I believed it would mask any noise my body might produce. I sat with my hand over the colostomy, as if holding my guts in, not daring to tell Libby the full story. Only later did I come to understand that in not revealing the full story I also cut myself off from support.

But that morning I knew only that I did not want anyone to know. I was absurdly grateful to Tracey for sitting close to me, for holding my arm as we walked down the street. She did not seem at all embarrassed, and I was impressed all over again by that dashing Callander style.

By the time I got back to the warehouse, however, I might have travelled as far as the moon. I was deathly tired, dumb with depression, exhausted by the effort of having to smile.

Excusing myself I returned to bed, longing for the oblivion of sleep.

Every morning I woke up and immediately felt my stomach. If I lay quietly in bed the stoma would begin its work for the day: a thin ribbon of shit curling quietly into the bag. I knew I wasn't supposed to feel anything but the experience felt oddly the same as passing shit the normal way, except that the sensation was centred around my belly.

The weirdest thing was getting used to lying in bed feeling myself shitting, without rushing to the toilet. While I was still in hospital I felt most comfortable sitting on the toilet while the stoma 'worked', but I was slowly training myself out of it.

In those first weeks a home based nursing service sent a stomal therapist out to check on how I was going. She told me that most normal bowels moved twice a day, but I was lucky if mine appeared to move only once. She supervised me putting on the pouch and wanted to take the stitches out around the wound because they didn't seem to be falling out as they should.

I didn't want her to touch me. I'd had enough of people coming at me with scissors and knives.

One morning I wrote in my notebook: *stay away from me, with your knives, your penises, your probes.*

A few real estate agents came to assess the warehouse. I always sat warily on a couch as far away as possible from anyone new, my hand over the stoma. A slick, good-looking agent told us we shouldn't lose any money, but we probably wouldn't make any either as it was generally not good practice to buy and sell a property within the year. Neither Les nor I cared about making money, we only wanted to get out without losing any.

We eventually decided on a particular real estate agency, and, because most property in Melbourne is sold at auction, we set a date for an auction a few months ahead.

Both Mum and Les thought it a good idea that I go up to Queensland in the meantime to recuperate. I knew they were worried about me.

I was having trouble putting one foot in front of the other. Melbourne, Queensland, the moon, it was all the same to me, for I hardly cared about anything.

I supposed I still loved Les and the boys, but it was a dull kind of love, as if buried too deep to locate.

True to her word, the hospital therapist sent out the mini-skirted ex-colostomy patient to see me. She wore a fluffy jumper over a little skirt, and sat down happily to tell me her medical history, a Crohn's Disease sufferer who had been in and out of hospital for much of her adult life. She was friendly, and I liked her lurid stories about bowel abscesses as big as footballs and a visit she had just made to another colostomy patient who was still in hospital.

'Honestly, Sue — I can call you Sue can't I? — well, honestly, there she was, crying her heart out because she'd had four inches of her bowel removed! I had to laugh, I've had three feet taken out of mine!'

She was one of those people for whom their medical dramas are the most exciting thing which has ever happened to them, and she talked about her various medical escapades with great flourish. I could see she was interested to know my full story, how my own colostomy had come about, for the vast majority of colostomies are a result of Crohn's Disease or bowel cancer.

I gave her a brief history, but I knew she was not satisfied. I wished I could have made her happy, but my pride prevented it; my pride recoiled every time she spoke of people never knowing attractive women like ourselves were disabled.

If I sound cruel, I do not mean to be. I honestly wanted her there, to ask her how I could live, to ask her how I could have sex with my own husband. I needed her, I needed her to tell me how to step back into my old life.

Mum was making us a coffee. I took a breath, and opened my mouth. 'Um,' I said. 'I ... I don't mean to be intrusive or anything, but what about sex? When you still had your colostomy did you and your husband have sex?'

I had barely ever talked about sex with my mother, yet here I was talking about sex with a mini-skirted stranger, and my mother was handing us both cups of coffee.

'Oh, Sue, that's not a problem!' she said with such abandon that I smiled. 'I even know one lady who made a little red satin heart sewn with lace to tie over her pouch whenever she and her husband made love. My husband never cared a bit!'

Mum smiled encouragingly.

I thought: *I am not a red satin heart kind of girl.*

I thought: *The Cosmo girl and her colostomy! How To Be Sexy With A Stoma!*

I thought: *I wish I could find the off button.*

Within weeks of getting home, Les's distance from me felt increasingly painful. He rarely touched me unless I asked him to give me a cuddle, he rarely looked me in the eye when I spoke to him. I was shocked at how estranged we had become, and asked him if he would agree to see the counsellor we had already visited once or twice. He said he would come.

In the room in suburban Melbourne it did not take me long to start crying. I saw Les's features stoically set; I saw his steady refusal to admit my emotional disarray. We talked about the colostomy. The counsellor asked Les how he would feel if it was Caspar who had one.

'I suppose I'd feel very sorry for him,' he replied.

We talked and talked, and I came to understand how Les was trying his best, that his way of dealing with the chaos surrounding us was to put his head down and keep going. He felt deeply attached to the notion that it was his responsibility to keep the family financially afloat, and felt that if he admitted chaos and fell apart too we would truly be lost.

We left the counsellor a little lighter, with Les agreeing to try to reveal his own fears as far as he was able, with myself agreeing to make less demands on him and to respect his different means of coping.

As we walked towards the car, Les took my hand.

Has the weight of all these lofty words allowed you to detect the pattern of my life by now? Can you tell that my writing is a mask I can put on and take off at will, that words can both reveal and deceive? I can be anyone when I write: kinder, smarter, tougher, more coherent certainly, a better woman.

But can you hear through these coherent words the reality of me screaming incoherently at a three-year-old Caspar and a twenty-three-month-old Elliot, telling them to shut up because I can't take any more fighting? Can you see me pushing my eldest son roughly down the corridor in an undignified way because he refuses to go to sleep when he is with me, even though he goes to sleep for every-body else? Can you see me push him so hard he falls over?

Did you believe me when I wrote that I had somehow managed to blend my writing life with my life as a mother, as far as I was able? Did you guess that the real story is much darker and more complicated, that I often feel frustrated and angry because I can no longer write in a composed and orderly way for uninterrupted blocks of time? That I cannot finish writing this, for example, because I currently have only one and a half days a week in which to do it, as well as dinner to cook, washing to hang out, a house to keep clean, children and shopping to pick up? Do you know that right at this moment I am writing as fast as I can before *Teletubbies* is over?

Writing sorts life into the appearance of one smooth surface, when the reality is that there are jagged days when I could murder myself or my children, and other drifting days when Caspar talks to flowers and the three of us practise butterfly kisses on each other. In reality I am the good mother and I am the bad mother: I am the good woman and the bad woman caught in the same net of skin.

Can any words I write hope to capture this tension? How can I possibly reveal to you every facet of my small personal sun? On the other hand perhaps my writing is the essence of me, a distillation of everything I am.

Do you sense through this distillation of myself that for the past few weeks while trying to finish writing these words I have been inexcusably bad-tempered with my children?

Can you appreciate the irony, me annoyed at my living flesh-and-blood children for getting in the way of a writerly reinvention of those very same children?

Did you guess that Les thinks I am insufferably precious about my writing, and that this memoir has become a no-go area between us? Do you see that in my role of writer reinventing the world I effectively render everyone around me mute?

Reader, you are reading only part of the story. *Mummy! Come here!*

Somehow we all managed to get on the plane to Queensland, the two babies, my mother and myself. I knew afresh I loved my children when Elliot began to have trouble breathing and his lips began to turn blue.

I unbuckled my seat belt even though we had not yet reached cruising altitude and rushed down to the air hostesses at the back of the plane. 'Sit down! Sit down!' they shouted over the noise of the straining engines, motioning me to a spare seat. An air hostess immediately ripped open a packet filled with eucalyptus oil or something, and placed it under Elliot's nose. 'Doesn't he need oxygen?' I shouted, and she picked up his fingers.

'Look at his fingernails. His colour's fine,' she said. 'If he was really in trouble his fingernails would have turned blue.'

As the seat belt sign was switched off and the plane levelled off I saw with relief that Elliot's breathing was returning to normal, that he was beginning to look with interest around him.

I was still shaking when I returned to my seat and I did not take my eyes off his fingernails for the rest of the flight. I did not think about the colostomy once.

Children do that to you, and it is both the joy and pain of them: they swallow up your woes, but they also consume the rest of you. In my experience small children are like ink on blotting paper, seeping out to the very edges of your life, leaving no white space whatsoever.

*

In Queensland the weaning of Elliot continued to go badly. He wouldn't take the bottle and the teat merely lolled around on his tongue. Now and then he took an exploratory suck, but more often he chewed the teat as if it were an especially designed teething ring. He didn't seem to understand that he was being offered a substitute nipple.

I was on the phone to either the Nursing Mothers or the Maternal and Child Help line practically every day. One expert suggested having my mother feed him so he could not smell my milk, but after half an hour my mother emerged from the loungeroom with an almost full bottle. 'He took one or two mouthfuls,' she said hopefully.

The truth was of course that I was hanging on as much as him, for when I fed him I did not want to let him go. I had come to see him as my little healer, for Elliot's happiness at being alive and breathing was almost palpable. He had recently discovered his toes and spent whole minutes gurgling at them with delight as if they were a kind of private joke. I took to calling him Mr Happy because he smiled at everyone and everyone smiled helplessly back. I felt for him an animal closeness, and could not bear the thought of my physical mothering coming to an end.

Yet I knew I had to give him up. For that is how it felt to me: as if I was giving up the whole of Elliot, rather than simply giving up breastfeeding him. I knew that when he finally took to the bottle our last physical link would be broken, that he would be moving out into the world, and away from me. I was full of sadness.

Yet I also knew I had to do it. I knew I wanted my body healed, as whole again as possible, but I also knew I was making a choice between two sadnesses. How sad would I be if my body never healed?

I finally spoke to a lactation counsellor who told me how to wean immediately, and gave her full support to my decision. 'It seems to me you don't have a choice,' she said, telling me exactly how to start.

Once I had finally made the decision I tried not to think about what I was doing. My mother fed bottles to Elliot and I refused him the breast; I drove to a nearby chemist to hire an electric breast pump. The idea was not to stimulate my milk supply this time (like all that pumping I did for Caspar), but simply to draw off the excess milk so my full breasts did not grow too painful.

Several times a day Mum tried to get Elliot to accept a bottle (and by now he was getting very hungry) while I went upstairs to the bedroom and pumped. I had to be careful not to pump too much, in case my brain got the message to keep filling up my breasts, but just enough to keep lumps and mastitis at bay.

Once I happened to see a milk drop at the end of my nipple and it looked to me exactly like a tear. I picked up the breast pump, void of tongue, and held it over my weeping breast.

I thought: *this sad pump for nobody.*

My nipples yearned for Elliot's suck.

One day I walked past a butcher shop and saw a pile of internal organs in the window. LIVERS AND HEARTS the sign read, and I immediately turned away.

I thought about the expression *Wearing your heart on your sleeve*, and wondered where it had come from.

Once I was driving home from my parents' local shops and a news report came on the radio about a surgeon being given some award for sewing a woman's face back on.

I thought: *they can sew someone's face back on but they can't stitch a woman's vagina up after a baby.*

I thought: *they can transplant human hearts, kidneys and livers, re-attach arms and fingers but they can't fix a tiny hole in an ordinary vagina.*

I thought: *just my fucking luck.*

One morning I was changing Elliot's nappy and it occurred to me that in a way the three of us were in nappies now: Caspar, Elliot and me.

My concept of the human body began to change. I looked at the bodies of supermodels in magazines, and thought only of glistening coils of bowels, shiny loops of lungs, the swish of blood. I saw that every face was incidental, beauty a chance meeting of genetic inheritance and current fashion, its variations of little consequence to that fixed and intricate plan beneath the skin. I thought about the body's endless blueprint, its anonymity and dependability, how rarely it displayed capriciousness.

What is a body exactly? What does it hide, this skin, this net of blood and water? What secrets does it cup? For the first time I feared my own body's power, as if it were a burning plane going down that I was trapped helplessly inside, clawing at the window.

The body's power, its scope, was suddenly revealed to me: only through my body's failures had I come to fully appreciate its power to *work*. What a mighty thing a body is, what powers it possesses: to stop life itself, to stop consciousness.

What a frail construction the body is, such a tremulous thing, easily felled. All that power halted so quickly by the gun, the car crash, the knife. All that power snuffed out in an instant, or killed slowly by malignant disease.

Power and frailty side by side, the faces each of us wear on the outside the merest of incidental envelopes.

In Queensland the sun was shining, but I could not feel it. Everything struck me as impossibly fragile: I feared for the health of my parents, Les, my children, myself. Princess Diana was killed in a car accident, and it only seemed to confirm how fine the line was between animation and extinction.

Watching the mangled car lifted up by a crane I felt a kind of free-floating anxiety about how much safety I personally had at my disposal. Could money not save you? Religion? Ideology? Love? Were all of us essentially defenceless?

Over those same few weeks we also learnt that June's prognosis was worse than everyone had imagined: the doctors had gone from diagnosing severe depression to some form of senile dementia. Tests were continuing.

June was still in hospital in Brisbane, and could recognise everyone, but sometimes she said odd things. Once my mother was visiting and complimented June on her nails.

'Your nails look nice. Who did them?'

June looked down at her hands. 'God,' she said.

The days turned to weeks and still I could not raise my head. One morning in the kitchen I shouted unforgivably at my mother for broadcasting to the whole world the intimate details of my colostomy, demanding how would she like it if I told everyone her bowel habits. I rushed crying from the kitchen, but even as I ran I knew I was behaving badly, acting like the worst kind of spoilt child.

(And if you think there is a contradiction between telling my mother off and writing of those same intimate details, you have not fully understood yet the difference between life and the creation of simulated life.)

Anyway, getting back to simulated life, I immediately returned to the kitchen to apologise, shamefully remembering all she had done and was doing, recalling all the hot baths she had run for me, the meals she had cooked, the nappies she had changed because I could not. I apologised to her, trying to tell her how angry I felt, with doctors, with the world, with God.

But most of all I was angry with my own body, for stuffing up.

Les came up for an extended stay, I guessed largely because he was missing the boys and not myself. The babies were thrilled to see him and together they went off on brief forays to the beach, to visit their big half-brothers Quintal and Ruben, to see their other Nan and Granddad. He and I made tentative steps towards each other, but it was as if each of us was engaged in a different dance.

My grandmother Molly made a special trip from Tweed Heads. I was pleased to see her, and one morning when she and I were sitting alone together at the large outdoor table I tried to tell her how I was having difficulty negotiating my way to the light.

'Oh, you won't have the bag on for long, Susie. What did the doctors say? Three months? It'll be over before you know it!'

I knew she was trying to help me but I still felt stranded in darkness.

I have a photograph of us standing together during this visit. She was eighty-two at the time and I was forty, and of the two of us she is clearly the more vibrant.

Now I have come to the moment where I heard that terrible howl for the second time, the sound of furious life shrieking at death. One afternoon at my parents' house I was putting Caspar down for a sleep when I heard a sound I could not identify. Immediately I lifted myself up on one elbow from the bed, my heart thumping, straining to hear. At first I thought it was Elliot, supposedly asleep in another room, but as I listened, every muscle in my body alert, I suddenly knew what the sound was and that I was about to learn something terrible.

I rushed from the room towards the sound, and found my mother in abject distress. My father was trying to comfort her but none of us had the right hands, the right words, the right power.

Tracey had just rung to say that June's diagnosis had finally been confirmed: she was suffering from CJD, or Creutzfeld Jakob Disease, popularly known as the human equivalent of Mad Cow Disease. No-one knew how she had got it, and only an autopsy could offer up the final clues.

She was going to die within weeks, or possibly days.

How is it that in the middle of all this grief I found the capacity to live?

How is it that one morning when everybody was out I took a chair into the garden and for the first time in many months felt the sun on my face?

One unremarkable morning I sat in a chair, noted that the swimming pool was still covered for winter, and all at once I realised that the air smelled sweet and the sun was blazing.

I sat up and looked into the unblemished blue sky. Without warning my eyes filled with tears: I was struck dumb by my own capacity to breathe in and breathe out.

I thought: *I am life, pulsing. My blood still moves, my lungs fill and collapse, I WORK.*

I thought: *I don't have full blown AIDS or brain cancer or numbered days, I have a small plastic bag stuck to my abdomen.*

I felt a kind of inner whoop, a silent roar.

I thought: *I am still here.*

I ran inside to phone Les to tell him that I loved him and that I wanted to come home.

16

The Measure of My Days

Lord, make me to know mine end, and the measure
of my days, what it is; that I may know how frail
I am.

PSALMS,
XXXIX, 4

Just as I began my life anew, June died. In late October her collapsing body finally gave in and she left us. Throughout her long leavetaking of the physical world her three daughters kept talking to her, massaging her with fragrant oils, stroking her warm hands, saying everything each of them needed to say. Until the very end her room was always full of close friends and family and flowers.

At her funeral men and women came from everywhere, people who had known her for years, girls she had only met once or twice. Those who could not come telephoned or sent flowers or cards or messages to be read. It was reported to me that at the wake my mother wore dark sunglasses as she spoke about her oldest friend, almost managing to finish her speech before her voice broke.

June's life was about connection: to her daughters, to Bob, the father of her children and whom she married twice, to her grandchildren, to her work and the world of ideas, to the everyday glory and squalor of love.

Her end was hard, just as much of her life was hard, yet at the same time there was transcendence. She was interested in the metaphysical knot of being alive, in the dignity of the struggle to live.

Like most of us, June was not unusually stoical or brave. I am fairly sure, for example, that she would have chosen for herself an easier end if she had been allowed a say in it.

Yet she was also the kind of woman who did not flinch from the knowledge that all of us are joined to the wheel, which continues to roll around and around, despite us.

My return to public life came in November when the now defunct television book show *Between the Lines* rang to ask if I would consider doing some dummy interviews while they auditioned several new presenters.

I didn't, of course, tell them that I would have hung upside down naked, colostomy bag swinging, for four hundred dollars. I had no money whatsoever, Christmas was looming, and Les saw before him only endless years of work and subsistence living, with no chance of going overseas again or even buying a decently made pair of shoes and some new clothes. We had no spare cash, no savings whatsoever.

While the producer tried to convince me to do the mock interviews, assuring me that it wouldn't be too taxing and all I had to do was talk about my books (she suggested *Hungry Ghosts* which hadn't received much publicity), I feigned hesitation. When I judged the moment was right I pretended to reluctantly agree.

Most writers will humiliate themselves for money. In reality, I was perfectly happy to answer the same questions over and over again in four separate interviews which I knew would never go to air.

Even though it was a hot day I wore my tightest pair of jeans, which I had found concealed my little lump beautifully, as well as masking any uncontrollable sounds. By this time I was fairly confident about the odd wayward belly fart. I idly wondered how sensitive the microphone attached to my T-shirt was.

As the cameras began to roll and I began the task of impersonating myself again, I placed my hand over my wound just in case and waited for the first question.

I thought of June, of going on, of the struggles yet to come.

I thought: *Here goes!*

I had not got the Literature Board grant for which I had applied, and I can't say I was surprised. My application had been a hasty one, and I suppose I was hoping the weight of the work which had gone before would get me over the line; it had not.

After eleven years of full-time fiction writing I finally admitted defeat. I could not live any longer with the whiff of Les's martyrdom, and I could no longer stand not having any money or savings of my own.

I tried not to feel as if I was making a choice between writing and my second marriage, but I have to tell you that sometimes it felt like that.

I began applying for jobs in journalism. I dared not think about the question of leaving my children.

In those rare moments when I could coolly analyse the position I found myself in I tried to ask myself some hard questions. What exactly was my moral duty in this situation? Could I justify any longer doing work which I loved but which brought in so few rewards? What of Les's needs? Was I as guilty as he believed of ranking my work and needs above his? Now that I had a family wasn't my first duty to them? I wondered if male writers had the same problems.

If truth be known, all through the years I had eked out a modest living through grants, publishers' advances, commissioned writing, creative writing teaching jobs, I had secretly believed that if it came to the crunch I could always go back to journalism. At the back of my mind there was a well-paying job waiting if I wanted it.

This wasn't as arrogant as it appears: I am a product of a particular time in history, and had grown up in an era where there were jobs to be had. As well as this, I had left journalism at a fairly high level, and had always assumed that at this level there would be a job of one sort or another. And surely my years of writing fiction would only enhance any journalism I might do?

But here comes the moment when life pulls the carpet from under my feet again. Here comes the moment when I found I had been harbouring false hopes all those years, where I learnt that my decision to return to journalism might not be mine to make.

After contacting every major broadsheet newspaper and magazine in Sydney and Melbourne I discovered I could not simply walk back into a job. A national magazine which had once run a four page feature on my work sent back a standard form letter. Most took months to reply in the negative.

An editor of a leading daily responded warmly that he loved one of my books and would give me a ring, but I never heard from him. *Vogue* was looking for health and medical stories and wondered if I might be interested in the occasional freelance piece.

In desperation I shamelessly contacted the producer of the aforementioned book show and suggested they might like to consider a fiction writer who was also a journalist for the presenter's job. They were surprised to say the least, and kindly declined my magnanimous offer.

Over the years I have grown used to humiliating myself in this manner. Only recently I had to ring a major newspaper no less than ten times to see about payment for a story published months before. It's harder than you think asking for money.

By the time I had exhausted practically every avenue in Australian journalism I have to admit I was dumbfounded. It was not that I considered myself a superlative catch, a big juicy name like Peter Carey or David Malouf, but certainly during my years out of the country I had nursed the idea that back in Australia my work was known in some circles at least. I believed that journalism was one of them.

At almost forty-one I learnt the reality of my untested beliefs: in the middle of my life I learnt that there was no safety net I could easily fall into, and that I had to go on walking the wire. Les tried to tell me not to take it personally, that the economic climate in general, and journalism in particular, had changed for the worse. I tried to believe him.

Not so many years ago I used to feel a keen hurt every time I met a devoted reader of Australian contemporary fiction who had never read my fiction.

The other day I happened to meet one such avid reader in a park with my sons. 'Oh, I've never heard of you,' she said. 'Do you use a pseudonym or is that the name you write under?'

I laughed. These days I am surprised to meet anyone who has read my work outside my family and friends. I have trained myself not to look down.

Do you want to know how Les and I learnt again how to dance that ancient dance? Do you want to know how we learnt the steps without the aid of a red satin lace-trimmed heart? For one day we found ourselves making the right moves again, without the need of lessons.

Despite all the conflict between us, our sensual life remains our true home, the one place where we speak wordlessly and most deeply. In this place our wounds are healed, the walls between us dissolve: it is the most intense erotic relationship of my life.

In this safe harbour I learnt how to trust again, how to offer myself up without fear. Through Les's patience and tenderness I learnt again the dance of my limbs.

For that, I thank him. Do not underestimate the full implications of this.

I put off going back into hospital for as long as I was able. I put it off because I did not want to know the worst, that if the fistula had not healed itself I would require another operation. I put it off because it's actually quite hard to organise a six week absence from your life while you recover and someone else stands in for you, getting your children up and dressed, cooking dinner, running the house, helping you to put on your own socks. I had to see if Les could get more time off work, if my mother could come down again or perhaps my in-laws, I had to cancel any outstanding work and social obligations.

I put it off, too, because I did not really want to undergo what is known as a flap repair if the fistula had not healed itself. In this procedure, done through the rectum rather than the vagina, a section of bowel is brought down to cover the fistula.

Essentially I had left the fanny specialists and gone over to the bum specialists: my new doctor was what was known as a colorectal surgeon. The Professor had effectively told me that there was nothing more to be done for me through the vaginal end, so to speak, so he was handing me over to the rectal specialists to see if they could fix me.

The first time I went to see the new specialist, a phlegmatic, likeable man of about my own age or perhaps a little younger, he asked me to lie on the examination table and plunged his gloved hand inside my colostomy like some kind of Filipino faith healer.

'Hey!' I said before I could help myself. Amazingly it didn't hurt.

'It's a good trick, isn't it?' he said, withdrawing his hand. 'You can get dressed now.'

In December I reluctantly went back into hospital, not knowing what the new doctor would find. Had my body been busy healing itself, secretly sewing itself back together without the help of a stitch? Had the weaning of Elliot caused my blood to rejoice?

Perhaps misfortune had laid its dirty fingers on me once again, picking me apart like so much rotten meat? I could not believe that as titular head of my bodily kingdom I did not know, that I could not tell if air was still coming out of my vagina. When the doctor asked me if I thought the fistula was still present, I had to tell him I no longer knew. My own body had turned into a secret.

The doctor informed me that he was going to do a thorough examination under anaesthetic to find out if I still had a fistula. If I did not, he would talk to me at a later date about reversing the colostomy as soon as possible. If he found that the fistula was still present, he would do the flap repair on the spot.

Not until I woke from the anaesthetic would I learn whether the fistula had healed itself. If it had not and I had required a repair I would have to wait until the repair had healed sufficiently and then wait until further tests on the efficacy of the repair before the colostomy could be reversed.

As I waited for the wardsmen to come and take me to theatre, I could hear my heart.

When I woke up I heard someone trying to tell me that the fistula was gone. It was the news I had been wanting to hear for so long, yet when it came it felt oddly anti-climactic. Even through my drugged haze I sensed that the mood was muted, not fully celebratory.

Within hours I learnt that even though the fistula had healed, my anal sphincter muscle was in extremely poor shape as a result of tearing through two births and repeated surgery.

The doctor was worried that if the colostomy was reversed I

would find myself incontinent. He wanted to talk to me about the possibility of repairing my anal sphincter muscle before he even considered a reversal.

I thought: *great, the fistula's gone and all I have to worry about now is shitting myself!*

I surprised myself by starting to laugh.

What a lovely word, *healed*, all slippery and loose. What a serendipitous notion, the body healing itself, its own best doctor. What propels this confluence of cells and blood and tissue, this luck? Did my heart do its job, cheering my blood on, willing the rest of me forward? Why me, and not June, whose autopsy results had revealed sporadic CJD, no known cause? I knew I was asking myself rhetorical questions.

I wished I could feel the full glow of the word, its sense of elation, but as the news finally sank in I felt only sadness.

I knew that there was more to come, more pain, more uncertainty, more waiting. I also knew that I was changed forever, whatever happened.

And what of Caspar through all this, through these long months of operations and recovery? What of my first born son through the tortuous weaning of my second son, through my griefs and small triumphs?

At two-and-a-half he was a self-possessed child, funny but slow to laugh, measured in his physical affection. Unlike his brother, he often shrugged off my physical advances, climbing into my lap only when he felt like it. I had learnt to wait for him, but he and I often clashed, for I could rarely get him to do anything he did not want to do. And as Elliot grew more mobile, able to interfere with Caspar's play, Caspar began to mark out territory and they began to fight in earnest.

It seemed to me that one day Caspar's speech was suddenly in place, and he began to make remarkable declarations. One morning I was drying myself after a shower when he came in, pointed to my pubic hair, and announced, 'Like a fire.'

I thought: *my darling, you cannot imagine how I have burned.*

And Elliot, that force of nature, that smiling boy sent to heal me? One evening, not long after he had turned one, I reprimanded him for climbing onto the shelves which held the television. 'You'll fall,' I said, prising open his tiny fingers before turning around to carry a load of clean folded washing down the hall.

As I walked the portable television crashed down on him, the shelves with it, the heavy lamp. He lay pinned to the ground, screaming hysterically, and in one leap I somehow hauled the television off from where it had fallen on his chest and scooped him up. He was still screaming so I knew he was alive: I could not tell how badly injured he was.

With shaking hands I gingerly inspected his chest, his head, trying all the while not to panic. As he began to vomit my brain registered that he probably had concussion and that I must immediately get him to a hospital. There was no blood.

Les happened to have the car and as I waited for the taxi I offered up pleas.

I begged: *cut my flesh again and again, sew me up, let me grow rotten but please do not lay a finger on my child.*

All the way in the taxi I pleaded with God, with the heavens, with life itself. I cradled my son as he slipped in and out of consciousness and knew without doubt I would rather my life gone than his, that I would endure any pain to save his.

After four hours of careful monitoring we were finally allowed home: mercifully Elliot had suffered only concussion.

In the new year of 1998 I began to teach novel-writing one day a week at the Royal Melbourne Institute of Technology University, frantically trying to finish this memoir as well.

This time in order to get the job I did not have to go through the rigours of a formal interview, but simply went in for a quiet chat with the two course co-ordinators, who also happened to be writers themselves. They knew my work, they knew writers needed money, and when they found out I had also taught writing classes in Hong Kong and London they offered me a job. Luckily for me, the RMIT course prefers to employ working writers as teachers, rather than academics.

I was being paid sessional rates, which is to say I was paid for the time I spent in the classroom only, and not for preparation or the reading and marking of manuscripts. I spent two full weeks, unpaid, preparing the first few lessons. It was hardly the return to lucrative employment I had envisaged.

I sometimes enjoy teaching, but I know I do not have the right nerveless temperament for it. In writing classes students bring their whole lives to their work, and I am always conscious that I am treading on tethered hopes. I find it a strain, achieving the right mix of encouragement, criticism and literary guidance, and I always feel slightly peeved that teaching drains so much of the energy that might otherwise go into my work. I never know how much to give of myself and I frequently give too much. I believe, too, that writers are born, not made.

As well as this, I have never been particularly good at knowing where the divide falls between private and public. I am too aware of the felt life behind the eyes, the revealing unconscious gesture, and while this skinned sensitivity helps my work as a novelist it can sometimes mean a somewhat peeled existence for me in the slapping cold air outside the pages of books. I sometimes find the real world exhausting.

That first morning as I stood in front of the class I tried to recall again where the line fell between private and public. If I had ever felt myself to be metaphorically devoid of skin, my body now seemed to mirror this discomfort.

I was thinking how my internal self had become external, how in a sense the private had become public. I was thinking of my raw private self, modestly covered, yet at the same time also profoundly exposed.

At RMIT one of the administrative staff in the department where I taught was a woman who was once a man. A complete artificial vagina had been constructed in her body where none had existed.

On bad days I thought: *they can turn a man into a woman but they can't fix me.*

On good days I thought: *my colostomy is my badge of honour, my medal of flesh. Every woman who has given birth wears this medal, only most are invisible.*

At the end of summer I wheeled Caspar and Elliot in the double stroller to a fete at an old people's home.

There was a band playing and the old men and women sitting in their wheelchairs tapped their slippered feet; some clapped their withered hands.

As I stood with my own hands resting on the stroller, the man standing next to me smiled at us.

Like me his hands rested on a kind of stroller too, only his took the form of a wheelchair: he was the adult son wheeling his infant mother.

I smiled back at him, then looked down at my boys' still heads. They were concentrating on the music and I suddenly understood that one day their grown hands might rest on such a handle too.

Their hands looked impossibly small.

In late May I organised substitute teachers for my last few classes before the mid-year semester break and returned to hospital for the sphincter repair. This time my parents paid for me to go into hospital as a private patient, ensuring that I would be able to nominate exact dates, have the doctor I wanted and get a private room. I was grateful, but I was also ashamed to find myself at forty-one having to accept my parents' money.

Before I went in, I underwent further tests aimed at giving my doctor more precise information regarding the state of the muscle. At a day clinic a series of probes was passed up my rectum, various small balloons inserted and then slowly pumped up with water, while a doctor told me to clench and unclench my bottom while he monitored the results on a screen.

Because of all the scar tissue the procedure was excruciatingly painful, and I found it hard not to leap up from the table and run from the room.

Unfortunately the nurse assisting these gruesome procedures was pregnant. She was young and healthy-looking, and I tried to make some comforting remarks about childbirth, assuring her that I was one of the worst case scenarios, one in a million, and chances were that nothing remotely unusual would happen to her.

'I know,' she said, unsmiling. 'I'm having an elective caesarean. After what I've seen here I wouldn't have a vaginal delivery if you paid me.'

I tried to concentrate on keeping my legs bent and blocking out the pain.

But I thought she had a point.

I will spare you yet another hospital visit, with its smells of over-cooked food, anti-bacterial soap, dying flowers. I will spare you the sound of IV drips beeping in the night, incessant calls for a nurse, the constant low buzz of televisions.

I will spare you the sight of me lying in bed, eating everything put in front of me like a bored passenger on a long haul flight. You only need know that I read stale magazines and watched the slate sky, noting that the trees were turning once again. I will confess though that I was terribly frightened (there was a chance the fistula would re-open) and each night I dreamed my body was invisibly festering. Turning on the light one night because I dared not sleep I idly picked up an old women's magazine and read the headline *The body seeks the truth*.

I wondered what truth my body was so tortuously seeking.

When I came home I couldn't sit down and I lived on my back or stood upright. I couldn't sit down on the toilet and took to peeing standing upright, holding a plastic bowl between my legs.

After perhaps three weeks, a month, I gingerly tried sitting on a cushion.

*

And that hinge between my legs, that vivid hinge on which my body seemed to pivot, without its grace I could not find my stride. I could not fall easily into a chair, nor rise from it again, I could not move my legs properly to walk. I hobbled, my shoulders hunched, and it seemed to me that the hinge on which my body depended was broken.

All natural movement was gone from me. That hinge suddenly seemed as essential as a heart, an instrument of propulsion, a vital spring.

My mother went home to Queensland yet again, very tired by now and in need of recuperation herself. I thought of Tracey and her sisters Fiona and Kerry, and how they were supposed to live cold in the world without June's unfailing heat. I myself was a middle-aged woman and yet I still supposed my mother to be as hot and as fixed as the stars.

Once I looked over at my mother while she was reading a book, her glasses perched on her nose, and for a moment she looked like a little old lady. *Oh, Mum*, I thought, *don't ever die. I couldn't bear it.*

My eyes blurred dangerously and I tried to speak of some of the things I was feeling.

'Oh, you just want someone to look after you,' she said, smiling, but I knew her well enough to also detect a certain tartness.

She was right, of course, though perhaps not in the way she supposed. I was a grown woman, yet I still felt my mother to be a kind of natural phenomenon, as unfailingly in my life as the waxing and waning of the moon. She represented to me nothing less than absolute love, the one place in the world I knew I could always find comfort.

I suddenly understood what a burden this might be for her, and wondered if my sons would one day feel the same way about me.

I thought: *what goes around, comes around.*

I thought: *I hope my puny self will one day rise like the moon.*

I was a one-woman catastrophe, a small ruined country, and my friends were suffering from compassion fatigue. How many times can you send flowers to various hospitals, issue Get Well cards? I found friends either did not fully comprehend how disabled I was after one of these procedures (and this is largely my own fault, because most did not know the extent of the problem), or else they felt uncomfortable around me, preferring not to dwell on my many absences from active life.

Once, not long after the last operation, I went to visit my dear friend Sandra. She suggested we start out on a walk but to my dismay we kept walking, on and on. I had not walked further than the top of the street since I had left hospital and as we kept going my discomfort and pain grew.

We hadn't seen each other for months, she was telling me about her life and I did not want to interrupt her. I walked on, hoping the moment would come when I could suggest stopping, sitting down at a cafe, or even heading home.

Finally, when it looked as though we would never stop, I had to ask if we could rest as I was getting tired.

'Oh, my God, Sue!' she said, mortified. 'I completely forgot about your operation! You look so well it went straight out of my head. I'm so sorry!'

Because my wounds were invisible to the outside world I had passed for someone who was unscathed.

*

After Les went back to work and I was still hobbling around like an old woman, Jillian from the book group brought around a week's supply of meals: frozen pumpkin soup, spaghetti bolognaise, beef casserole. She said Maryann or Jane would be around the following week with another week's supply.

Every woman in the group had babies or very small children, no spare time, jobs, relationships and houses to run, and I knew exactly what cooking extra meals for another family would have cost them.

I was speechless and tears sprang up in my eyes.

Such kindness re-attached me to life.

When I went back to class I wished I had brought a pillow with me. I stood up for much of the day (not for the whole eight hours: I saw students individually and also took an extended break between classes to rest in the sick room).

The students all hoped I had enjoyed my long break and that I was nicely recovered.

As Susan Sontag has written, there is the kingdom of the sick, and the kingdom of the well, and neither can envisage the other.

'Is that your hospital, Mummy?' Caspar asked the other day as we passed one of Melbourne's public hospitals.

Now, every time I look up at a hospital, I know that it is peopled by those expelled from the kingdom of the well. I know there are eyes looking out at the turning trees, residents of that singular grey land longing for the light.

Spare a thought for them, won't you, those residents of that ghostly mirror kingdom.

*

It was too much, carrying on teaching (the sheer volume of manuscripts I had to mark was overwhelming), trying to recuperate, trying to finish work on this memoir. I still had only two days of childcare and the teaching work was swallowing every hour. I knew I had to give up teaching if I was going to finish the book on time. I had already passed the agreed date for delivery of the manuscript, but the publisher kindly agreed to an extension of several months.

But if I gave up teaching I would have no money to pay for childcare, and if I had no childcare I would be unable to finish the book on time.

After discussions with Les, we agreed that I would give up teaching (and the income), and that for a finite period of three or four weeks he would pay for full-time childcare while I finished the manuscript. The idea was that when I had finished, the publisher would then release the final outstanding money owed to me, making me financially viable once again, at least for the short-term.

But life got in the way again: Les's back went into painful spasm (he was effectively rendered immobile and a doctor eventually diagnosed arthritis), the children got viral chest complaints and woke up repeatedly, night after night, the manuscript continued to grow and grow, and everyone gave up asking if I had finished yet. My left eyelid started to droop again.

Les was in agony, angry about me working so hard, unhappy about the boys being in full-time care (as I was too). I was unbelievably stressed, trying to finish writing about my children so I could be with my children, panicked because I knew that at any moment Les would declare the full-time period of childcare to be over, and I knew it would take forever to finish then. Each night in bed I tried to plan in my head what I would write the next morning so I did not waste one precious minute in starting. I was writing in air.

As you can see, we were incendiary, burning hot, and it was only a matter of seconds before we were aflame.

I think you know the rest of the story.

17

The Pleasure of Being

The pleasure of being, that forgotten, unknown pleasure to so many mortals; this thought so sweet, this happiness so pure, *I am, I live, I exist*; is alone enough to convey bliss, if we remember it, if we enjoy it, if we know the value of it.

FRANÇOISE DE GRAFFIGNY, *LETTERS WRITTEN BY A PERUVIAN PRINCESS*

I now live in a house with a fence with Les and our sons. Our house is more early Beverly Hillbillies (before they left the farm) than Beverly Hills, for our garden is shamelessly unkempt and paint is peeling from the front door.

I will tell you about two things you will find in the spare room: my writing desk and Les's drum kit. In these two details you have everything you need to know: evidence of a shared life, of clashing needs, of the willingness of the fox to lie down with the hare. I will leave it to you to decide who is the fox and who is the hare but anyone who has tried to share the same air with another breathing creature will recognise it is possible to be both fox and hare at once.

The computer I used to write much of this book (I ended up discarding pen and paper as I went to save time) is now in the boys' room, where they use it to play rudimentary computer games. It does not have a mouse so their fingers clumsily hit the same keys on the keyboard where I used to type, except they are moving imaginary motorbikes down raceways in Brazil and Japan.

I don't need it anymore as it happens, for I have a better computer with a mouse at the office where I now go to work. For the moment I have no need of fiction, for in the year 2000 I am once again a woman of the working world, with a regular salary and a train to catch. For the past year I have been the editor of a Saturday feature section of a Melbourne newspaper, with money once again in my purse. It is an interesting job, devoted to books, arts and what are known curiously as 'ideas', and I am grateful to have it. For one thing it has allowed me to pay off the hefty personal loan I took out in January 1999 to pay for the colostomy reversal.

Did I tell you I am now all of a piece, that I am no longer inside out? Did I tell you that my once captured rosy flesh has dived beneath my skin again like a joyously released fish, never to be exposed to the air until my body's final decay? That when I share a bath now with Caspar and Elliot they ask when my sore tummy will get better (they don't yet understand about the permanency of scars) and that Elliot sometimes traces the thick scar with his finger and once said that it looked like a lizard? I had a slight infection in the wound following the operation which caused the healing tissue to buckle oddly: the scar is wide and slightly raised and you can clearly see where the stitches once were.

But the strange thing is this: I have already begun to forget. It is as if my body remembered its old self, its old reconfiguration and, as in a dream, it simply closed over where once it had been open. I live now with the sense of something always behind me, some shadow I might glimpse if I turned fast enough. Yet I also live as if I survived something: I taste the air, I drink from the cup, I savour the sweet flesh at the necks of my children.

Did I mention that they are already slipping away? That each day takes them further and further away from their baby selves and that only a few traces of their old grub selves remain? At four and three both still wear nappies at night and only Elliot still wishes to take his meals from a high-chair. Both long ago refused to wear bibs.

Caspar goes to kindergarten four days a week and Elliot for two sessions. Ever since I went to work full-time, Les has gone part-time, working three days a week and caring for the boys the other two days. On the days when both Les and I are working the children are looked after by a gentle Vietnamese woman in her neat house, where she teaches them Vietnamese songs and how to make origami aeroplanes.

Caspar is now four years old, although he remains sceptical of the calendar. The day after his fourth birthday he turned to me with a sorrowful face and said, 'My birthday didn't work. I'm still three.'

But you are four my darling, and soon you will be five, soon you will be fifteen, twenty. Soon you will slip away into your own life.

For the moment though you are still mine, as if we share the one life. I still help to dress you, to identify your right and left feet, to wipe your skinny bottom and act as your interpreter in the world. You still don't know the meaning of words, the connections between things, but you soon will. I can see the intelligence behind your eyes beginning to make links, that the principle behind the alphabet will soon be clear to you. You are scaling the letter A yet you already know everything you need to know: I am your mother, Les is your father, you are our loved first son.

Caspar still occasionally appears to me like a complicated recipe that I must follow carefully. He is a sensitive child and the world must be explained to him slowly and cautiously. If I rush past him, as is my wont, his reactions are sometimes violent: more than once I have stopped the car and threatened to leave him by the roadside. I am often my most violent self with him too and our relationship is a volatile one: he is the child I broke myself upon in learning to scale the cliffs of motherhood and this experience is embedded in us like a code.

But if Caspar and I are sometimes in tangled communication, Elliot's workings seem transparent to me. I intuitively understand his motivations, the well-springs of his rages, in ways that are obscured from me in Caspar. I can always calm Elliot, talk him down as it were from the window ledge. He is an energetic boy, tireless, always jumping, from trees, from cubby-houses, from sofas. His passion is wrestling and he is always ready to be tickled. He mimics everything that Caspar does and is sometimes frustrated because Caspar can do things that he cannot. They regularly fight as if partners in the world's worst marriage and at these moments I wish I could effortlessly walk out the door.

Yet almost every day I learn something new from them and

almost every day they also make me laugh. In the bath once Caspar looked at me and said, 'Do spiders eat breakfast?'

It is true that for children the world exists only as a kind of sensation. One morning Elliot kept sniffing me before I realized that he was trying to sniff the flowers on my shirt. And once, when Caspar was sick and I was trying to find out if he was getting any better, I asked how he was feeling. 'Red,' he replied.

Not so long ago I was sitting with Caspar in the sunlight under a window when he announced, 'Mummy, you've got cobwebs in your hair.'

I fumbled around trying to extricate them (I had been out in the garden which is full of spiderwebs) before I realised that he was referring to the silver hairs in my head which have recently multiplied.

For Christmas last year Caspar got a new book about escaping circus elephants from Nana Helen and Grandad in Queensland. In the story, the little boy who rescues the elephants finally takes them home.

'Maybe *we* could take the elephants home, Cappy,' I said. 'Where would we put them?'

'Mummy!' he said. 'You can't take the elephants out of the story!'

Reader, please give this point your consideration as you finish this book, these carefully chosen words re-creating for public consumption some of the most private and intimate moments of my life.

Consider this, won't you, as you come to the end: *You cannot take the elephants out of the story.*

It seems to me that since I gave birth to my sons my life in every way has become broader, deeper, richer. They have drawn from me my best self, and while physically I am not the woman I once was, I am a better woman.

I know for certain now that I am fully attached to life and love, and that life and love have fully attached themselves to me. My arms are full.

I no longer have the sense that my true life is just out of reach, if only I could find my way to it.

I am fully here, at last.

It is true that I have arrived late in my life, when the dust of age is already in my mouth and cobwebs are in my dark hair. I have arrived only to learn that my days are numbered.

Still, if by chance you should happen to meet me, do not be afraid to look me in the eye. I promise you that all my organs are now demurely back in their rightful place and I will not hold your hand too long.

I have been to a strange country, but have no fear, for what I brought back with me will not be visible to your naked eye. I am carrying personal information that my body is a template, its circuits already in place, coded to my hidden final moment. I know now that I am already written, fully composed.

Eight days before the Mexican painter Frida Kahlo died, when her body was in the last stages of disintegration, she painted her final work. After she had painted her name in blood red paint, she wrote in capital letters VIVA LA VIDA (Long Live Life).

Like her, I intend to keep holding fast, to Les, to my children, to my pen, to all my difficult and abundant loves.

I am a soldier in life's army of love, marching in the never-ending present moment.

When I am gone my sons will walk on, taking the best of me with them.

And listen to this: reader, I made it to the end.

Acknowledgements

Thanks is too paltry a word to convey the debt I owe to the following people. Each in their own way lit the flame which allowed me to go on.

Margaret Connolly, my agent and friend, spoke to me on those black days when my fears threatened to engulf me. She kept talking to me when she had laryngitis, when there was dinner to be cooked, when I called her for the fourth time in a single day. When I thought everything was falling apart, she took pains to show me what treasures I had to live for.

The book group I serendipitously stumbled upon has made me feel that Melbourne is finally my home. Above all, I thank Maryann Ballantyne for inviting me to join, Janine Ballantyne, Marian Costelloe, Margaret Neal, Jillian Graham and Jane Sawyer for all their kindness and support. I am lucky to know them.

Lynne Segal's unfailing generosity kept me supplied with books and the articles relating to Louise Erdrich and Michael Dorris which came at a critical point in the writing of this memoir. Craig Cranko wrapped up a complete Brio trainset for Caspar which gave me time to write while he played with it on the floor beside me.

Amy Witting helped more than she can ever know when I was at my lowest point.

My parents-in-law, Bill and Helen Webb, offered unfailing support and love, as did my grandmother, Molly Cooney.

Jane Palfreyman of Random House showed me compassion,

patience and generosity in advancing money I technically should have received much later. Margaret Sullivan had enough faith to inspire me to begin. Jamie Grant's sensitivity and sense of aesthetics was much appreciated.

The doctors who oversaw my body's breakdown and recovery did so with empathy and kindness and I thank them. Allan Souter taught me how much I needed to learn.

Of the many nurses who acted as my legs and arms I thank them, each of them shining beacons to their profession. Jane Connolly also lent her light.

Liz Foulkes and Anna Bradbury were generous in time and spirit and Carolyn Woodford and Rahnee Squire-Wilson lent capable and kind hands when they were needed. From my early days of motherhood I thank Jann Zintgraff, Robin Barker and Judy Condie for their humour, knowledge and compassion in teaching me what a baby needs to live.

My dear friends Emma Felton, Sandra Hogan and Susan Oakenfull made me feel the world was kind again. Helen Quinn and Graeme Coop did too.

Tracey Callander and Simon Palomares and Lee and Jay Palomares-Callander showed me that in life connection is everything. I thank Kerry and Fiona Callander, June's elder and younger much loved daughters, for allowing me to share in this book some of their mother's most private moments.

To June Callander herself especially, thank you, wherever you are.